# PROFESSIONAL STUDIO TECHNIQUES
# DESIGN ESSENTIALS

*Third Edition*

Luanne Seymour Cohen

Adobe Press
San Jose, California

International Standard Book Number: ISBN: 1-56830-472-2

Library of Congress Catalog Card Number: 98-85102

Printed in the United States of America

first Printing: May 1999

**Trademarks**

All terms mentioned in this book that are known to be trademarks or service marks have been appropriately capitalized. Adobe Press cannot attest to the accuracy of this information. Use of a term in this book should not be regarded as affecting the validity of any trademark or service mark.

**Warning and Disclaimer**

Every effort has been made to make this book as complete and as accurate as possible, but no warranty or fitness is implied. The information provided is on an "as is" basis. The author and the publisher shall have neither liability nor responibility to any person or entity with respect to any loss or damages arising from the information contained in this book.

# Acknowledgments

I read many acknowledgment pages before I sat down to write this one. Typically, there is a lot of well-deserved gratitude to researchers, testers, and advisors at the beginning, and somewhere down near the bottom of the page, there is a loving nod to the spouse and/or children of the author. I think the best should come first in this case. I can't thank enough my best friend and husband, **Rick**, for his support, love, and patience during the production of this book. Honey, you're the greatest! My children have been really good sports while their mom was ignoring them and working away. They've also been wonderful models, artists, and creative inspirations for me. Thank you, **Jessica** and **Charlie**. I love you.

This book has been a team effort. Thank you so much for helping me:

**Sandy Alves**, book designer, sushi lover, Illustrator expert, and now Photoshop 5 color expert. Thanks for not quitting when you got your full-time job.

**Barb Terry**, my wonderful editor and cheerleader and a great listener. You were so kind to me while you slashed my copy that I never felt a thing.

**Chris Nelson**, publisher, deal maker, and all-around great guy. You are the publishing world's Bert Monroy. I'll miss you.

**Gay Allen**, my other best friend. Thanks for all the hikes, listening to me rant and rave, and being there to help out whenever I needed you.

**David Cohen**, Adobe products expert and color expert extraordinaire. Your color separation and printing advice was invaluable.

**Elizabeth Keyes**, for her excellent and very professional book design advice.

**Caleb Belohlavek**, for rising above and beyond the call of duty to help his wife, Sandy, finish production of this book. You are a king among husbands.

**Pascal** at **Adjacency**, for letting me use his technique for making big, efficient GIF images.

**Lisa Trail**, for dropping everything to help us complete this project.

**Tanya Wendling**, for helping me keep perspective. You're fabulous, darling!

Thank you to the following people who contributed material, tested the techniques, gave technical advice, or inspired me: **Ted Alspach, Paul Asente, Russell Brown, Sandee Cohen, Chris Cox, Jack Davis, Jennifer Eberhardt, Katrin Eismann, Bruce Fraser, Mark Hamburg, Barry Haynes, Jessica Helfand, Andrei Herasimchuk, Aren K. Howell, Jill Jones, Julieanne Kost, Gary Kubicek, Michael Mabry, Jeff Schewe, Steve Weiss.**

Thanks also to our bad dog, **Sam**, whose frequent antics got me out of the chair and away from the computer for a good stretch.

# About the author

**Luanne Seymour Cohen** has been a graphic designer for the last 22 years. Some of the Silicon Valley companies she has worked for include Atari, Apple Computer, and Adobe Systems. She was a Creative Director at Adobe for twelve years where she created package designs and illustrations and produced a variety of collateral materials for Adobe and its software products. She also developed and designed the Adobe Collector's Edition products. One of her responsibilities was to work closely with the engineers as an advisor during the development of Adobe's graphic software. She wrote and art directed the first two editions of *Design Essentials* and another book in the series, *Imaging Essentials*. Some of her award-winning work has been shown in *Communication Arts*, *Print* magazine, the *Type Directors Club*, *Print* casebooks, and the AIGA annual. She has taught workshops and classes all over the world including Stanford University, Kent State University, University of California at Santa Barbara, Anderson Ranch Arts Center, Center for Creative Imaging, the Thunder Lizard Photoshop and Illustrator conferences, and California College of Arts and Crafts. An avid quilter for more than 32 years, she also teaches classes and writes articles on digital quilt and fabric design. In 1995, she published a book, *Quilt Design Masters,* with Dale Seymour Publications/Addison Wesley. This book is used in elementary school classrooms to teach mathematical principles. She and her family live and work in the San Francisco Bay Area.

# Contents

# Introduction

**Design Essentials, Third Edition** shows how to produce traditional graphic and photographic effects using Adobe Photoshop, Adobe Illustrator, and Adobe ImageReady software. This book, like the other books in the Professional Studio Techniques series, does not attempt to describe the features of these software programs. Instead it is a quick, how-to recipe book for artists familiar with the basic tools and commands in the programs.

Because the software has changed so much between the publication of *Design Essentials, Second Edition* and now, all of the techniques are new or have been completely rewritten. Each technique has been tested extensively by professional designers, Web page designers, illustrators, teachers, photographers, and novice users. Even though I make the assumption that the reader has a basic working knowledge of the software, I have included an appendix that reviews the basic shortcuts and commands that I use every day with these programs. I've also included a recommended reading list. You can find an overwhelming number of Photoshop and Illustrator books to help you learn more about these very versatile programs. My list includes only books that I think offer accurate, well-researched, and well-designed information.

*Design Essentials, Third Edition* covers the most recent versions of the Adobe software for both Macintosh and Windows platforms: Adobe Photoshop 5.0, Adobe Illustrator 8.0, and Adobe ImageReady 1.0. Many, but not all of these techniques can be used with older versions of the software. The required software for each technique is indicated beneath the technique title. Look for the shortcuts in the appendix. When keys are indicated in the text, I use a slash (/) to separate the Macintosh and Windows key needed. For example:

> "Press the Option/Alt key when clicking on a button" means
> **Macintosh** users press the Option key.
> **Windows** users press the Alt key.

# 1 Drawing

# Custom borders

*Adobe Illustrator 8.0 or later*

One of the most useful things you can create with the Illustrator pattern brush is a border. Pattern brushes offer you the option of having corner designs that look different from the side designs. You also don't have to worry about calculating the size of the tile to fit your particular rectangle because Illustrator offers three Pattern Brush fit options. If you want to customize one of the pattern brushes provided in the several libraries that came on the CD, simply drag the tiles out of the Brushes palette onto your page and change the artwork to your taste. Then follow steps 7 through 14 to resave the tiles.

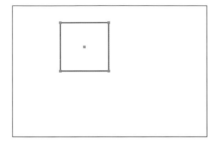

**1.** Select the rectangle tool and create a square large enough to contain the border corner artwork.

It doesn't matter what the fill and stroke are because this square will eventually become a guide.

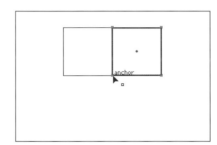

**2.** With the selection tool, click on one of the left corner points and drag the square to the right, pressing Shift + Option/Alt as you drag. Once the left corner point aligns with the right one, release the mouse button and then the Shift and Option/Alt keys to create a copy.

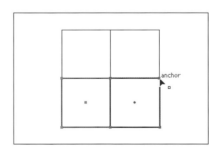

**3.** Select both of the squares, click on one of the corner top points, press Shift + Option/Alt, and drag the squares straight down. Once the top corner point aligns with the bottom one, release the mouse button and then the Shift and Option/Alt keys to create copies.

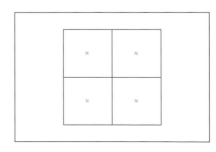

**4.** Select all four of the squares and choose View > Make Guides.

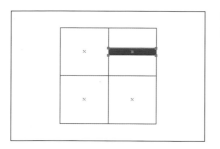

**5.** Create the artwork for the sides of the border in the upper-right square guide.

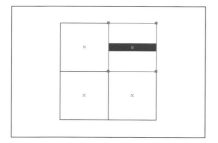

**6.** Select the rectangle tool and create a square the same size as the square guide. Fill and stroke the square with None. Choose Object > Arrange > Send to Back.

This invisible square will become the bounding box for the side pattern tile. It will also help you align the side tile with the corner tile.

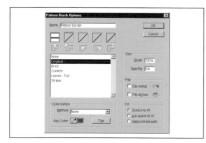

**7.** Select both the side artwork and its invisible bounding box. Choose New Brush from the popup menu in the Brushes palette. Select Pattern Brush as the type. The side tile artwork will appear in the Side Tile thumbnail. If you want the border to remain the same color, choose None for the Colorization method. Click OK.

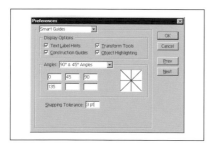

**8.** Choose File > Preferences > Smart Guides to set the Display Options. Turn on all of the Display Options. Then choose View > Smart Guides and make sure they are turned on.

You need to use these to be sure the tile art and corner art align perfectly.

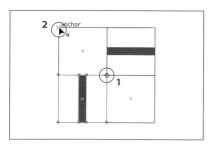

**9.** With the side tile artwork still selected, choose the Reflect tool from the toolbox. Click once on the bottom left corner of the selected artwork (1). Press the Option/Alt key and then click a second time on the upper-left corner of the top left guide box (2) to create a copy.

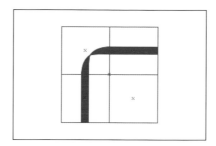

**10.** Create the corner artwork. Use the Text Label Hints, Object Highlighting, and Construction Guides as aids in matching the points of the outer corner design to the side tile design. The side tile should flow seamlessly into the outer corner tile.

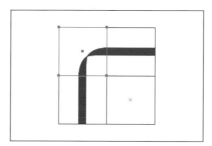

**11.** Repeat step 6 to create an invisible bounding box for the outer corner design.

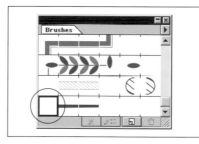

**12.** Select the outer corner tile artwork and its bounding box. Option/Alt-drag it into the Brushes palette and position it over the outer corner section of the new pattern brush you created in step 7. Release the mouse button, then the Option/Alt key when you see the thick black border appear. Click OK in the Pattern Brush Options dialog box.

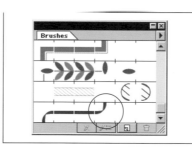

**13.** Repeat step 12 for the inner corner design except Option/Alt-drag the design into the inner corner section in the Brushes palette. Usually the outer corner design works as the inner corner design as well. To create an inner corner for non-symmetric borders, return to step 10. Rotate the outer corner tile art 90° and adjust it to match the side tile. Continue with step 11.

**14.** Once you've defined the sides and corners of the pattern brush, test it. Draw a shape and click the pattern brush name in the Brushes palette.

Notice in the example that shapes without corners were painted only with the side tile design. Corner tiles appear only on paths with corner points.

# Dashed line effects

*Adobe Illustrator 8.0 or later*

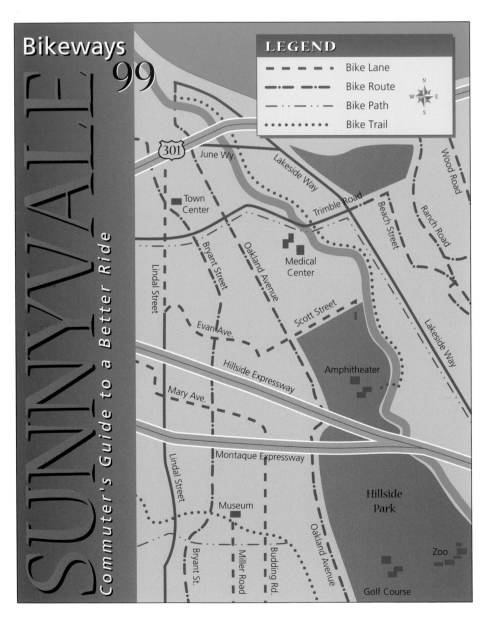

You can generate a variety of useful and decorative effects by varying the dash patterns of your lines and then layering the lines. The following charts provide recipes for just a few examples. To create a single-line effect in Illustrator, select the line, open the Stroke palette, (Window > Show Stroke), and enter the values shown in one of the effects. To create the layered-line effects, paint the stroke using the values shown in the first row of the recipe, copy the line, choose Paste in Front, and paint the copy using the values shown in the next row. Repeat this procedure until all layers have been created and painted. When you have achieved the effect you want, group the lines together.

| Single Lines | Stroke Color (%) | Stroke Weight (points) | Line Cap (style) | Dash Pattern |
|---|---|---|---|---|
| | 100 | 2 | Round | 0, 2 |
| | 100 | 2 | Round | 0, 4 |
| | 100 | 2 | Round | 0, 6 |
| | 100 | 2 | Round | 0, 10 |
| | 100 | 2 | Projecting | 0, 3 |
| | 100 | 2 | Projecting | 0, 4 |
| | 100 | 2 | Projecting | 0, 6 |
| | 100 | 2 | Projecting | 0, 10 |
| | 100 | 2 | Butt | 10, 6 |
| | 100 | 2 | Butt | 12, 12 |
| | 100 | 2 | Butt | 14, 6 |
| | 100 | 2 | Butt | 20, 6 |
| | 100 | 2 | Round | 20, 10, 0, 10 |
| | 100 | 2 | Round | 10, 5, 0, 5, 10, 12 |
| | 100 | 2 | Round | 8, 4.5, 0, 4.5, 0, 4.5 |
| | 100 | 2 | Projecting | 15, 6, 5, 6 |

| Single Lines | Stroke Color (%) | Stroke Weight (points) | Line Cap (style) | Dash Pattern |
|---|---|---|---|---|
| | 100 | 4 | Butt | 0.3, 8 |
| | 100 | 8 | Butt | 0.3, 4 |
| | 100 | 12 | Butt | 0.3, 6 |
| | 100 | 16 | Butt | 0.3, 10 |
| | 100 | 10 | Butt | 4, 3 |
| | 100 | 18 | Butt | 3, 4 |
| | 100 | 12 | Butt | 0.3, 2, 0.3, 6, 5, 6 |
| | 100 | 15 | Butt | 2, 4, 10 |

| Layered Lines (values shown by layer) | Stroke Color (%) | Stroke Weight (range) | Line Cap (style) | Dash Pattern |
|---|---|---|---|---|
| | 100 | 20 | Round | 0, 24 |
| | 90 | 18.25 | | |
| | 80 | 16.5 | | |
| | 75 | 14.5 | | |
| | 65 | 13.0 | | |
| | 60 | 11.0 | | |
| | 50 | 9.25 | | |
| | 40 | 7.50 | | |
| | 35 | 5.75 | | |
| | 25 | 4.00 | | |
| | 20 | 2.25 | | |
| | 10 | 0.5 | | |
| | 100 to 10 | 20 to 0.5 pts | Butt | 10, 30 |
| | 10 to 100 | 10 to 0.5 pts | Round | 30, 24 |
| | 100 | 25 | Butt | 2, 2 |
| | 80 | 20 | | 2, 2 |
| | 60 | 15 | | 2, 2 |
| | 40 | 10 | | 2, 2 |
| | 20 | 5 | | 2, 2 |

| Layered Lines (values shown by layer) | Stroke Color (%) | Stroke Weight (points) | Line Cap (style) | Dash Pattern |
|---|---|---|---|---|
| | 100 | 7.5 | Butt | 2.5, 7.5 |
| | 60 | 5 | | 5, 5 |
| | 20 | 2.5 | | 7.5, 2.5 |
| | 100 | 8 | Butt | Solid |
| | 20 | 6 | | Solid |
| | 100 | 6 | | 10, 10 |
| | 80 | 12.5 | Butt | 7.5, 2.5, 2.5, 2.5 |
| | White | 7.5 | Butt | 5, 10 |
| | 40 | 5 | Round | 0, 15 |
| | 30 | 10 | Projecting | 0, 13.5 |
| | White | 5 | | 0, 13.5 |
| | 100 | 2.5 | | 0, 13.5 |
| | 100 | 10 | Round | 0, 10 |
| | White | 5 | | 5, 5 |
| | 60 | 15 | Round | 0, 15 |
| | White | 15 | Butt | 1.5, 2.25, 1.5, 9.75 |
| | 100 | 8 | Projecting | 0, 12 |
| | White | 9.5 | Round | 0, 12 |
| | 30 | 1 | Projecting | 0, 12 |
| | 100 | 13 | Round | 0, 14, 0, 20 |
| | White | 11 | | 0, 14, 0, 20 |
| | 100 | 6 | | 0, 14, 0, 20* |
| | Black | 20 | Butt | Solid |
| | White | 15 | | 15, 2.5 |
| | Black | 10 | | 12.5, 5 |
| | White | 5 | | 2.5, 15* |
| | White | 2.5 | | 10, 7.5 |
| | Red | 30 | Round | 0, 35 |
| | White | 25 | | 0, 35 |
| | Red | 20 | | 0, 35 |
| | White | 15 | | 0, 35 |
| | Red | 10 | | 0, 35 |
| | White | 5 | | 0, 35 |

*move line down 2.5 points

# Quick 3-D boxes

*Adobe Illustrator 8.0 or later*

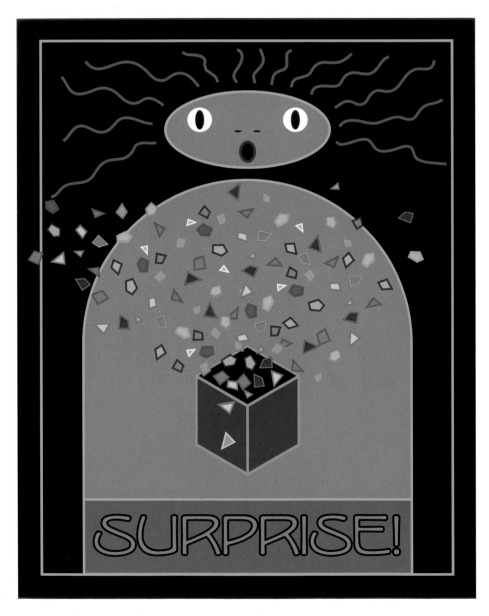

Illustrator's Smart Guide feature allows you to quickly create objects at specific angles without rotating and shearing. Follow this technique and you'll learn how to create a three-dimensional box. Then you can use this technique to create a vast array of three-dimensional objects. Try making your drawings using some of the other angle choices available in the Smart Guides Preferences. If you find that the Smart Guides are elusive and hard to find as you move the mouse around, change the Snapping Tolerance preference to a higher value.

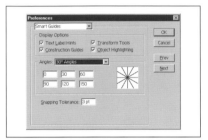

**1.** Choose View > Smart Guides to turn them on. Then choose File > Preferences > Smart Guides. Select 30° Angles for the Angle type. Turn on all four of the Display Options. Finally, adjust the Snapping Tolerance, if desired.

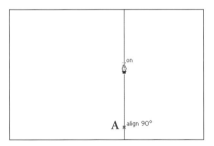

**2.** Choose Window > Show Info. Select the pen tool and click to make the bottom corner point (point A). Without clicking the mouse button, move the pen straight up along the Smart Guide 90° line until the Info palette displays the desired height of the front panel edge.

In this example, the height is 48 points.

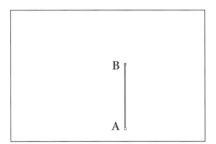

**3.** Click the pen at the desired distance to establish point B.

Make sure you click when the Smart Guide is displayed and when it indicates that the line is aligned at 90°.

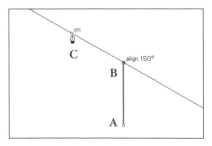

**4.** Drag the pen tool, without pressing the mouse button, at an angle along the 150° Smart Guide. Look at the Info palette and when the pen is positioned at the correct distance for the width of the front panel, click to establish point C.

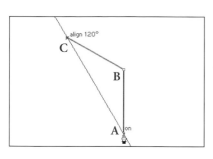

**5.** Drag the pen down to point A to let Illustrator know that you want to align your next point with this corner point.

If you don't perform this step, you will be guessing where on the 90° guide to place the bottom back corner point.

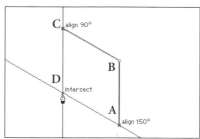

**6.** Drag the pen away from point A along the 150° Smart Guide. When you get close to the 90° guide that is aligned with point C, move the pen slowly until you see both guides appear at once. There should be a text label that says "intersect." Once you see this, click to establish point D.

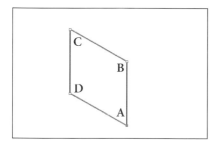

**7.** Click on point A to close the path.

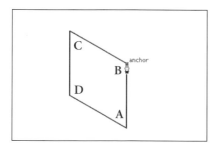

**8.** Deselect the front panel shape. Position the pen tool over point B and click to start the edge of the top panel.

Deselecting is important here because the pen tool will automatically remove the point if you click over a point on a selected path.

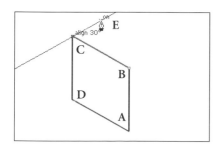

**9.** Click again on top of point C. Drag the pen out along the 30° Smart Guide until the desired distance is achieved. Click the pen to establish point E of the top panel.

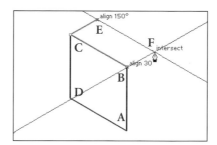

**10.** Drag the pen down to point B and then along the 30° Smart Guide until the intersection point appears. Click to establish point F.

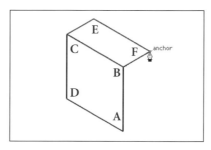

**11.** Click on point B to close the top panel shape. Deselect the top panel and position the pen tool over point F. Click to establish the first corner point of the side panel.

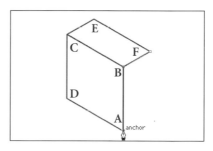

**12.** Position the pen over point B and click once. Move the pen down and click on point A.

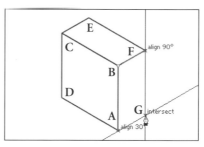

**13.** Without clicking, drag the pen up to point F and then drag down the 90° Smart Guide until you reach the intersection with the 30° Smart Guide. Click to establish point G at the lower-right corner of the side panel.

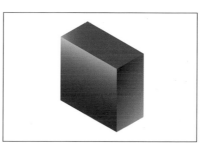

**14.** Click on the bottom front corner point to close the side panel shape. Fill each panel with different colors or gradients to emphasize the three dimensions, and then save the file.

# 3-D packages

*Adobe Illustrator 8.0 or later*

You learned how to quickly draw a three-dimensional box on page 8. But what if you have a flat package design that needs to be transformed from two dimensions into three? Use Adobe Illustrator's precision tools to create isometric, axonometric, dimetric, and trimetric views from your two-dimensional artwork. The chart at the end of this technique provides the precise values needed for each type of three-dimensional drawing.

**1.** Create a flat view of your package, and then group the artwork for each panel. Using the examples shown on the facing page, choose the three panels on which you need to produce a perspective view and position them as indicated.

The three panels will be scaled, sheared, and rotated using the intersection of the three panels as the point of origin.

**2.** Select the top panel. Choose the scale tool and Option/Alt-click the intersection point to set the point of origin. The Scale dialog box opens.

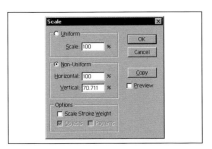

**3.** Select the view you want to create from the chart on the facing page. Click the Non-Uniform Scale option and enter the appropriate Vertical scale value for the top panel.

In this example, I entered the value for the Trimetric 2 view.

**4.** With the top panel still selected, choose the shear tool and Option/Alt-click the intersection point. Enter the appropriate value for Horizontal Shear from the chart on the facing page.

In this example, I entered 45°.

**5.** Select the rotate tool and Option/Alt-click the intersection point. Enter the rotate value indicated in the chart and click OK.

This step causes the top panel to appear to recede into space.

**6.** Repeat steps 2 through 5 for the front panel. Be sure to use the numbers indicated for the front panel in the chart.

**7.** Repeat steps 2 through 5 for the side panel, using the corresponding set of numbers in the chart.

**8.** If the panels are stroked, zoom in very close on the corner joints to see whether the corners extend past the intersection point, as shown in this illustration. Identify which panels have this problem.

**9.** To fix the corners, use the direct-selection tool to select the panel edges. Choose the Round Join option in the Stroke palette. To enhance the three-dimensional effect, paint the panels with slightly different shades and tints. Save the file.

In this example, I lightened the colors on the top panel and darkened the colors on the side panel.

| View Style | | | Vertical Scale | Horizontal Shear | Rotate |
|---|---|---|---|---|---|
| Axonometric | | Top | 100.000% | 0° | -45° |
| | | Front | 70.711% | -45° | -45° |
| | | Side | 70.711% | 45° | 45° |
| Isometric | | Top | 86.602% | 30° | -30° |
| | | Front | 86.602% | -30° | -30° |
| | | Side | 86.602% | 30° | 30° |
| Dimetric | | Top | 96.592% | 15° | -15° |
| | | Front | 96.592% | -15° | -15° |
| | | Side | 50.000% | 60° | 60° |
| Trimetric 1 | | Top | 86.602% | 30° | -15° |
| | | Front | 96.592% | -15° | -15° |
| | | Side | 70.711% | 45° | 45° |
| Trimetric 2 | | Top | 70.711% | 45° | -15° |
| | | Front | 96.592% | -15° | -15° |
| | | Side | 86.602% | 30° | 30° |

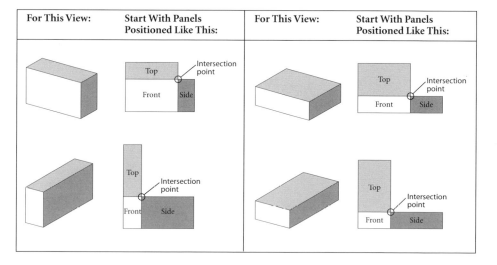

| For This View: | Start With Panels Positioned Like This: | For This View: | Start With Panels Positioned Like This: |
|---|---|---|---|

# 3-D pie charts

*Adobe Illustrator 8.0 or later*

The graph tool in Adobe Illustrator lets you create two-dimensional pie charts using data imported from a spreadsheet or entered directly. Once you are sure that the data will not change, you can customize the chart by making it three-dimensional. I recommend saving the original flat pie graph in a separate file just in case you need to make changes to it later. In this technique, I simply darken the sides by adding black, but I recommend trying gradients to add even more dimension.

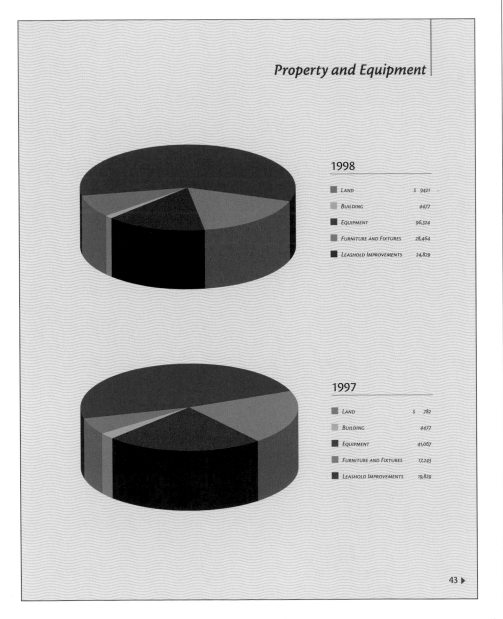

**Property and Equipment**

### 1998

| | | |
|---|---|---|
| ■ | LAND | $ 9421 |
| ■ | BUILDING | 4477 |
| ■ | EQUIPMENT | 96,324 |
| ■ | FURNITURE AND FIXTURES | 28,464 |
| ■ | LEASHOLD IMPROVEMENTS | 24,829 |

### 1997

| | | |
|---|---|---|
| ■ | LAND | $ 782 |
| ■ | BUILDING | 4477 |
| ■ | EQUIPMENT | 41,067 |
| ■ | FURNITURE AND FIXTURES | 17,243 |
| ■ | LEASHOLD IMPROVEMENTS | 19,829 |

43 ▶

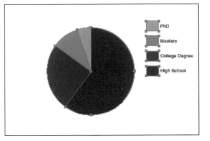

**1.** Create a pie graph with the graph tool using imported or input data. Select each pie segment and paint with the color of your choice. Select the graph and choose Object > Ungroup to release the first level of grouping. You will get a message stating that if you ungroup the graph, it will lose its connection to the graph data and type. Click OK.

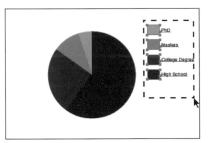

**2.** Choose the direct selection tool and cut and paste the graph key onto a different layer. Lock or hide the layer until the 3-D pie is finished. Turn on Snap to Point and Smart Guides under the View menu.

If you don't want to keep the graph key for later use, delete it.

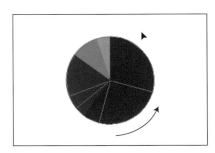

**3.** Select the pie and then choose the rotate tool from the toolbox. Rotate the pie so that none of the sides of the pie wedges are horizontal or vertical.

**4.** Select the pie, and double-click the scale tool in the toolbox. Select Non-Uniform and enter a Horizontal value of 100% and a Vertical value of 40%. Click OK.

This "flattens" the top so that it appears to recede into space.

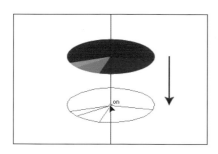

**5.** Choose the selection tool and, with the pie still selected, begin dragging the pie downward along the 90° Smart Guide. Press the Option/Alt and Shift keys to make a copy. When the copy is positioned at the desired depth, release the mouse button and then the Option/Alt and Shift keys.

This copy will be the bottom of the pie.

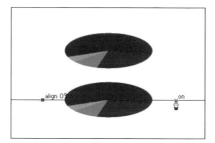

**6.** Select the pen tool in the toolbox. Position the pen over the center point of the bottom pie but do not click the mouse yet. You will see the word "anchor" appear. Move the cursor to the left of the pie and click to establish a point. Now move the cursor (without pressing the mouse button) along the 0° Smart Guide to the right of the pie and click to create a straight line.

**7.** Select both the line and the bottom pie. Choose Window > Show Pathfinder to display the Pathfinder palette. Click on the Divide button to slice the pie in half with the line you just created.

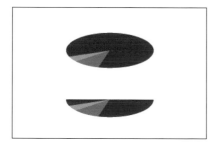

**8.** Use the direct-selection tool to select the upper half of the sliced pie, and then delete it.

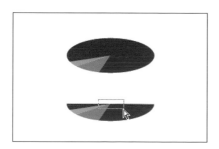

**9.** Drag a marquee around the center point of the bottom pie half with the direct-selection tool. This selects the endpoints of each remaining line in the pie half. Delete the points.

You will use the remaining part of the pie to build the base and sides of the three-dimensional pie graph.

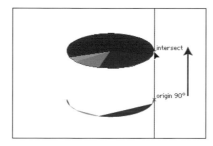

**10.** With the lower pie parts still selected, drag upward along the 90° smart guide. Press the Option/Alt and Shift keys and drag until you see the "intersect" hint appear. Release the mouse button and then the Option/Alt and Shift keys to leave a copy.

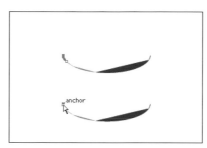

**11.** Select the top pie, which is still grouped, and choose Object > Hide Selection. Select the remaining edge shapes and choose Object > Ungroup. Using the direct-selection tool, select the two leftmost endpoints on the two leftmost curves.

**12.** Choose Object > Path > Join to connect the points. Then select the rightmost points in the left shape and choose Object > Path > Join to connect them.

You have created the side wall of the right-most shape.

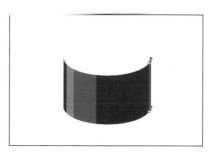

**13.** Choose Object > Lock to make selecting the adjacent shape easier. Repeat steps 11 and 12, working from left to right until all the side shapes have been created.

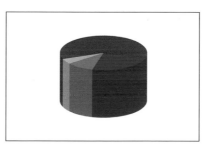

**14.** Choose Object > Show All to view the pie top. Paint the side shapes a slightly darker color than the top shapes. Add type and a graph key if desired.

In some cases, the top may be slightly off-register with the sides. If so, select the top, zoom in, and reposition using Snap to Point to align the points.

# 3-D bar charts

*Adobe Illustrator 8.0 or later*

The graph tool in Illustrator creates flat, basic, unsophisticated graphs. But it is useful for calculating the correct ratio or size of the graphic elements. In this technique, start with a basic bar chart and create your own three-dimensional bar design. The third dimension adds a little more visual interest, but be careful. The purpose of a bar chart is to represent information that can be easily compared. Simple bar designs work best!

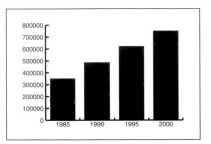

**1.** Create a grouped or stacked bar chart. Choose the View menu and turn on both Snap to Point and Smart Guides.

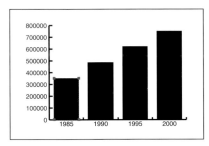

**2.** Use the direct-selection tool to select the smallest column in the graph. Copy it to the Clipboard and deselect the shape.

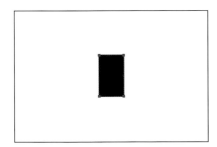

**3.** Create a new layer and call it *Graph design*. Select that layer and paste the rectangle onto it. Hide the layer with the graph on it.

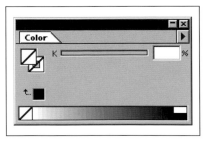

**4.** Paint the rectangle with a stroke and fill of None. Copy this version to the Clipboard.

This will become the bounding box for your bar design.

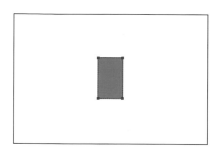

**5.** Choose Edit > Paste in Front to paste a copy of the bounding box directly on top of itself. Paint the rectangle with the color you want for the face of the three-dimensional bars.

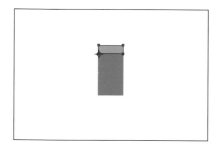

**6.** With the rectangle still selected, choose the scale tool and Option/Alt-click the upper-left corner point of the rectangle. Choose Non-Uniform scale and enter a Horizontal value of 100% and a Vertical value of -20%. Click Copy. Paint the top with a different color.

This shape will become the top of the three-dimensional bar.

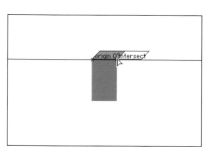

**7.** Select the Shear tool and click once on the same upper-left point you clicked on in step 6. This sets the point of origin. Then click on the right top point of the top rectangle, press and hold down the Shift key, and drag along the 0° smart guide. Release the mouse button and then the Shift key when you are happy with the shear angle.

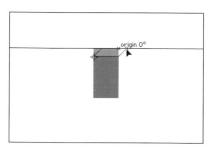

**8.** Choose the selection tool. Click one of the left corner points of the sheared top rectangle and drag to the right. Hold down the Shift and Option/Alt keys to make a copy and constrain it along the 0° smart guide. When you reach the corresponding right corner point, release the mouse button and then the Shift and Option/Alt keys.

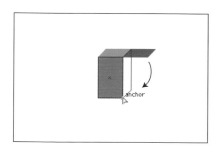

**9.** Use the direct-selection tool to select the two rightmost anchor points of the copy you just made. Click and drag the front right point down until it snaps to the lower-right corner point of the bar. Paint the side of the column with a different color.

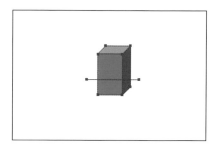

**10.** Use the pen tool to draw a horizontal line that intersects the column design. Position it between the top and bottom corner points. Select the line and the bar design and choose Object > Group.

This line will be the "sliding boundary"—a line below which the design will be vertically scaled in a graph. The area above the line won't change.

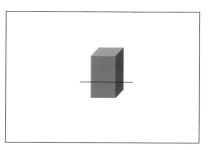

**11.** Use the direct-selection tool and select only the horizontal sliding line. Choose View > Make Guides.

The guide is grouped with the bar design. Even though you might have Lock Guides turned on, it will still be selected when the group is selected.

**12.** Select the group and choose Object > Graphs > Design. Click the New Design button. Click the Rename button if you want to name the design something other than the default name automatically applied. Click OK.

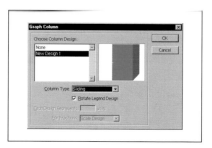

**13.** Hide the *Graph design* layer in the Layers palette. Show the layer containing the bar graph. Select it and choose Object > Graphs > Column. Select the new column design and choose Sliding as the Column Type. Click OK.

**14.** Choose View > Hide Guides to evaluate the results.

Adjust the layering of the axis lines or bars if necessary. Use the direct-selection tool to select the shapes or lines and use the Arrange menu to reposition them. You can also change the type style and copy at this point.

# Shaded spheres

*Adobe Photoshop 5.0 or later*

You can easily create shaded spheres using the gradient fill tool in Photoshop. This technique shows you how to create a basic sphere in steps 1 through 5. If you want to add more subtle shading to the sphere, continue with steps 6 through 14. Because the shading is on a different layer than the sphere, you can change the color, layer mode, and opacity as often as you want. Try making several versions of shaded areas and layering them for even richer shadows.

## COMMON CHEMICAL COMPOUNDS

| Compound | Name | Molecule model |
|---|---|---|
| $H_2O$ | Water | |
| $NH_3$ | Ammonia | |
| $H_2O_2$ | Hydrogen Peroxide | |
| $CO_2$ | Carbon Dioxide | |

**The basic sphere**

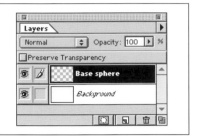

**1.** Open a new or existing file and create a new layer. Name the layer *Base sphere*.

**2.** Select the elliptical marquee tool. Press the Shift key and draw a circle.

Hold down the Option/Alt key to draw the circle from the center point.

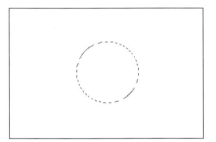

**3.** Select the radial gradient tool from the toolbox. Choose Window > Show Options to display the Radial Gradient Options palette.

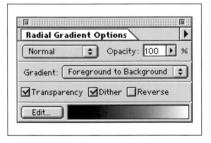

**4.** Click on the Edit button to display the Gradient Editor. Create a new gradient and name it *Sphere*. Use a highlight color at one end and a shadow color at the opposite end. Place a pure color at the 50% point on the gradient slider.

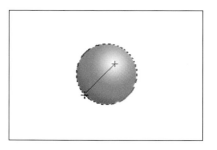

**5.** Position the radial gradient tool inside the circle selection at the point where you want the highlight. Choose *Sphere* as the gradient. Click and drag to the edge of the selection and release the mouse button. Deselect the sphere.

If you are satisfied with the result, save the file. To add more shading or reflections, continue.

### Adding more shading

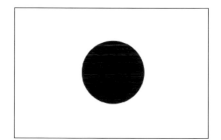

**6.** Duplicate the *Base sphere* layer and name the new layer *Blurry sphere*. Turn on the Preserve Transparency option.

On this layer, you will construct a soft shadow that will lay over the base sphere.

**7.** Choose Edit > Fill and fill the layer with Black.

Only the non-transparent areas of the layer will be filled with black. I used black here so that it was easy to see against the colored sphere.

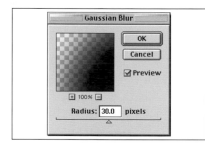

**8.** Turn off the Preserve Transparency option. Select Filter > Blur > Gaussian Blur and adjust the Radius amount until the sphere is at least as soft as the example shown here. Click OK.

The Radius value you need depends on the resolution of your image and the size of the sphere.

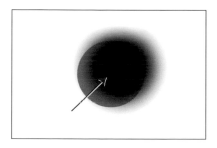

**9.** Select the move tool from the toolbox. Move the *Blurry sphere* layer in the direction of the sphere highlight. The area of the sphere that is revealed will eventually become the area that is shaded.

**10.** Create a new layer and name it *Shading*.

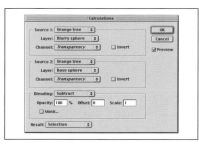

**11.** Choose Image > Calculations. Source 1 should be the *Blurry sphere* layer with the Channel set to Transparency. Source 2 Layer is set to *Base sphere,* and its Channel should be set to Transparency. Choose Subtract as the Blending mode and Selection as the Result. Click OK.

The Preview should display the area that will be shaded on the sphere.

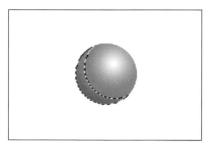

**12.** With the selection still active, hide the *Blurry sphere* layer. Select the *Shading* layer if it is not already selected.

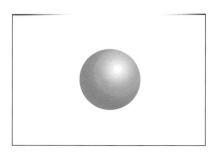

**13.** Select a color from the Color palette for the shading. Fill the selection with the color, and then deselect.

Don't worry if the color looks too flat or light. Try to pick a color that is reflective of something near the sphere (for example, green leaves on a tree), or try using the complimentary color of the main sphere color.

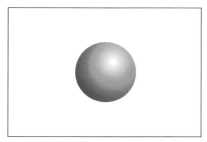

**14.** Change the layer mode to Multiply. Adjust the opacity if necessary.

You can quickly change the color by turning on the Preserve Transparency option for the *Shading* layer. Then choose different colors and fill the layer until you are happy with the result.

# Perspective grids in Photoshop

*Adobe Photoshop 5.0 or later*

You can create a perspective grid in Photoshop that helps you match the perspective of imported graphics and images to that of the background image. This technique is especially helpful with images that contain strong perspective lines. To create the grid, you draw paths that define the vanishing points and horizon line of the image. Then you draw grid lines for positioning and sizing the imported artwork. Once the grid is created, you distort the imported image to align with the grid lines. Don't worry if the guidelines reach outside of the image; the pen tool displays outside the image in full screen mode.

**1.** Open the background file.

**2.** Option/Alt-click the New Layer button in the Layers palette and name the layer *Guidelines*.

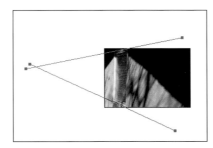

**3.** Select the pen tool from the toolbox. Click the Full Screen Mode with Menu Bar button at the bottom of the toolbox. Zoom out and draw two paths that follow the perspective lines in your image. Use the direct-selection tool to pull out the endpoints of the lines to a point where they intersect.

This is referred to as a vanishing point.

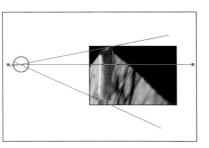

**4.** Create the first point of a new line, hold down the Shift key, and click the second point to draw a horizontal line. Use the direct-selection tool to move it until it intersects the vanishing point.

This is the horizon line.

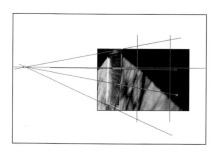

**5.** Draw additional guidelines to help create the perspective for positioning additional images or graphics.

In this example, I drew additional lines as guides for type that I will place on the building wall.

**6.** Select the *Work Path*, if it is not already selected, in the Paths palette, and then choose Save Path from the popup menu. Name the path *Perspective grid*.

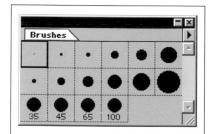

**7.** Select the pencil tool from the toolbox. Choose Window > Show Brushes to display the Brushes palette. Select the smallest of the Default brushes.

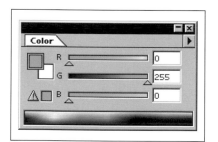

**8.** Choose Window > Show Color to display the Color palette. Select a very bright color to stroke the guidelines with. Choose something that will show up well against your background file.

The guidelines will not be printed; they will only be used for reference while building the image.

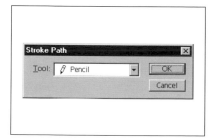

**9.** Make sure the *Guidelines* layer in the Layers palette is selected. With the *Perspective grid* path still selected, choose Stroke Path from the Paths palette popup menu. Make sure the pencil tool is selected as the Tool and click OK.

**10.** Choose Turn Off Path from the Paths palette popup menu so you can view the stroked lines. If the lines don't show up well on your image, continue with step 11. If the lines show up well, skip to step 12.

**11.** Select a new color in the Color palette. Turn on the Preserve Transparency option for the *Guidelines* layer. Choose Edit > Fill and fill the layer with the new foreground color. Continue trying this until you find a color that contrasts well with your image.

**12.** Create, place, or paste the image to be transformed into perspective.

**13.** Choose Edit > Free Transform. To distort freely, press the Command/Ctrl key while dragging one of the corner points to its desired location. Use the guidelines as references to position each of the corner points of the transform bounding box. Once the image has been scaled and distorted to fit the guidelines, press Return/Enter to perform the transformation.

**14.** Hide or delete the *Guidelines* layer. If necessary, adjust the layer mode or opacity of the transformed image to make it work with the background layer. Repeat steps 5-14 for any other objects that you add to the image.

# Perspective grids in Illustrator

*Adobe Illustrator 8.0 or later*

This technique shows how to use guidelines and smart guides to create perspective drawings. First, you'll set up the perspective grid and create the flat shapes that appear on the picture plane. Then you'll draw the sides of the objects along the gridlines and create any receding copies of the elements within the object using the scale tool. The final steps in the technique show how to create blends for repeating horizontal or vertical details.

### Drawing objects in perspective

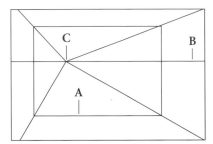

**1.** Create a simple 1-point perspective grid. First draw a rectangle to denote the picture plane (A) and a horizon line (B). Then decide where the vanishing point (C) will be. Draw straight lines from the vanishing point past the corners of the rectangle. The lines should intersect the corners of the picture plane.

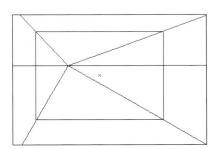

**2.** Select the lines and rectangle and choose View > Make Guides.

To open a more complex, pre-made grid, use the File, Open command, go to the Illustrator application folder, and follow this path: Sample Files > Template Samples > 1ptPerspectiveGrid.ai.

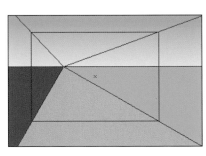

**3.** Create the background shapes. Remember to use the horizon line guide when creating skies and earth or floors and walls.

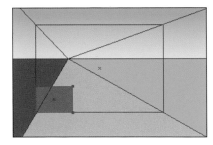

**4.** Create a new layer for the object(s) that sit above the background shapes. Check the View menu to see that Snap to Point is turned on. Create and fill the shape for the front plane of the first object in your drawing. Draw a flat shape with no distortion.

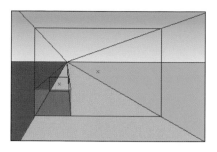

**5.** Select the pen tool and draw a line from one of the corner points to the vanishing point. While the line is still selected, choose View > Make Guides. Repeat this process for all of the key points and angles on the front plane.

In this example, I added guides to help create the bottom, back, and right side of the box.

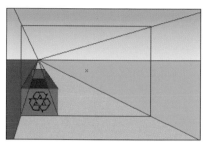

**6.** Draw the sides of the object using the guides. Paint them with colors slightly different from the front shape. Repeat steps 4 through 6 for each new object you create. Continue with step 7 to transform objects into perspective.

In this example, I chose Object > Arrange > Send to Back to position the sides behind the front.

### Transforming in perspective

**7.** To create multiple shapes that recede toward the vanishing point, create the frontmost shape with guidelines and select it. Choose View and turn on Smart Guides.

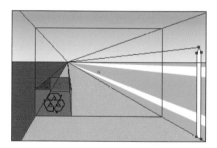

**8.** Select the scale tool, and then click the vanishing point once to set the origin point. Move the cursor to a point on the selected shape that intersects one of the guides. Drag the point along the guideline toward the vanishing point; press the Option/Alt key. Release the mouse button and then the Option/Alt key to make a copy.

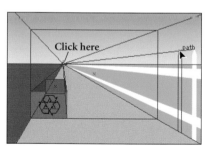

**9.** To make additional receding copies, choose Object > Transform > Transform Again for as many copies as you need.

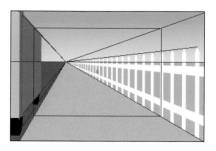

### Blending in perspective

**10.** To create evenly spaced lines or shapes on the sides of objects, draw the frontmost shape using the perspective guidelines.

In this example, I drew a shape instead of using a stroked line so that the top and bottom of the line would be angled properly.

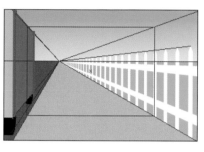

**11.** Use the scale tool as instructed in step 8 to create a smaller copy of the line or shape at the far end of the surface.

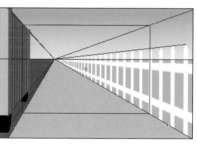

**12.** Select both lines or shapes and choose Object > Blends > Make.

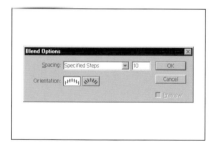

**13.** With the blend still selected, choose Object > Blends > Blend Options. Select Specified Steps for the Spacing and try different numbers of steps until you are satisfied with the effect. Click OK.

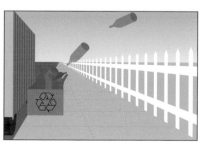

**14.** Add other objects to complete the illustration using the guides, the vanishing point, and the horizon line as aides in their construction.

I recommend using layers for each different object. Include that object's guidelines on its layer to keep the drawing organized.

# Seals, stars, spheres, and links

*Adobe Illustrator 8.0 or later*

The techniques in this section are quick, easy ways to draw little graphics often needed by designers and illustrators. The Scalloped seals and Three-dimensional stars techniques use a combination of Illustrator commands. The Quick spheres technique is a fast way to make a sphere without a 3-D drawing program. You can't overlap stroked shapes easily, so turn them into compound paths first. Then create interlocking shapes with just a few clicks on the Pathfinder palette.

## Scalloped seals

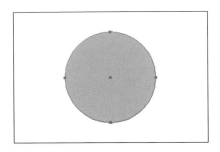

**1.** Select the ellipse tool, press and hold down the Shift key, and draw a circle. Holding down the Shift key makes it a perfect circle.

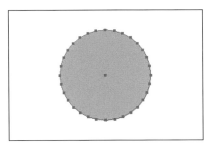

**2.** Choose Object > Path > Add Anchor Points. Reapply the Add Anchor Points command until you have the number you want.

In this example, I applied the command three times.

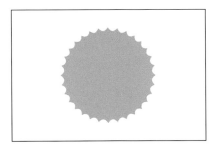

**3.** Choose Filter > Distort > Punk & Bloat. Place a check in the Preview box and enter a negative number if you want the points on the outer edge of the circle. Click OK.

In this example, I used a value of -5%.

***Variation:*** For a softer effect, use a positive value when applying the Punk & Bloat filter.

In this example, I applied the Add Anchor Points filter twice and used a value of 5% with the Punk & Bloat filter.

## Three-dimensional stars

**1.** Select the star tool and click once in the document. Enter 4 in the Points field and click OK.

In this example, I used a value of 40 points for Radius 1 and 20 points for Radius 2.

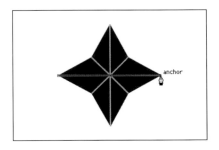

**2.** From the View menu, turn on Smart Guides and Snap to Point. Select the pen tool and draw horizontal, vertical, and diagonal lines across the star between the anchor points. Use the smart guides to help you locate the anchor points.

It's a good idea to stroke the lines with a contrasting color to check alignment. The stroke color will disappear in the next step.

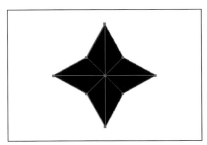

**3.** Choose Window > Show Pathfinder to display the Pathfinder palette. Select the star and all the intersecting lines. Click the Divide button in the Pathfinder palette to slice the star into separate shapes.

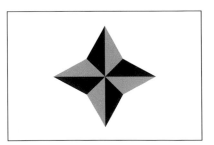

**4.** Hold down the Shift key, choose the direct-selection tool, and select every other triangle in the star. Fill them with contrasting colors.

For the best results, use a dark color for the shaded areas and a lighter value for the highlighted areas.

### Quick spheres

**1.** Select the ellipse tool, press the Shift key, and drag to create a circle.

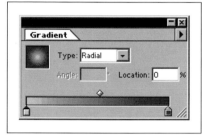

**2.** Choose Window > Show Gradient to display the Gradient palette. Create a new gradient with the highlight color on the left side of the gradient slider and the shadow color on the right. Choose Radial as the Type.

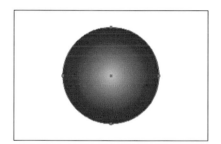

**3.** Select the circle, if deselected, and fill with the radial gradient.

By default, the highlight color (the leftmost on the gradient palette slider) is in the center of the circle.

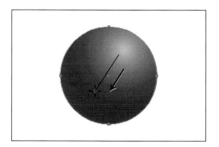

**4.** Select the gradient tool and then drag from the point where you want the highlight to the point where you want the shadow to begin.

**5.** Move the diamond above the gradient slider to increase or decrease the amount of highlight in the sphere. Deselect.

In this example, I moved the diamond from the 50% position to the 60% position to increase the size of the highlight.

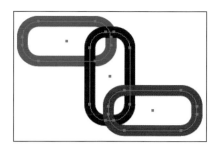

### Interlocking stroked objects

**1.** Create the stroked objects that you want to link.

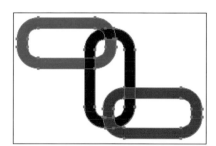

**2.** With the objects still selected, choose Object > Path > Outline Path.

Applying the Outline Path command defines each stroked path as a filled compound path.

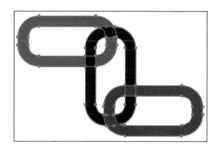

**3.** With the objects still selected, choose Window > Show Pathfinder to display the Pathfinder palette. Click the Divide button to define the overlapping color areas as separate shapes.

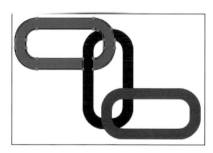

**4.** Determine how the links should be arranged visually to create the interlocking effect. Use the direct-selection tool and Shift-select the shapes you want to fill with one color. Click the Unite button in the Pathfinder palette to join the selected shapes into one shape. Paint with the appropriate color.

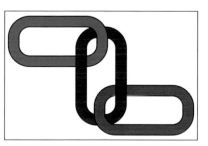

**5.** Repeat step 4 for all the interlocking objects in your artwork. Adjust the fill and stroke attributes of the objects if necessary.

# Global map symbols

*Adobe Illustrator 8.0 or later*

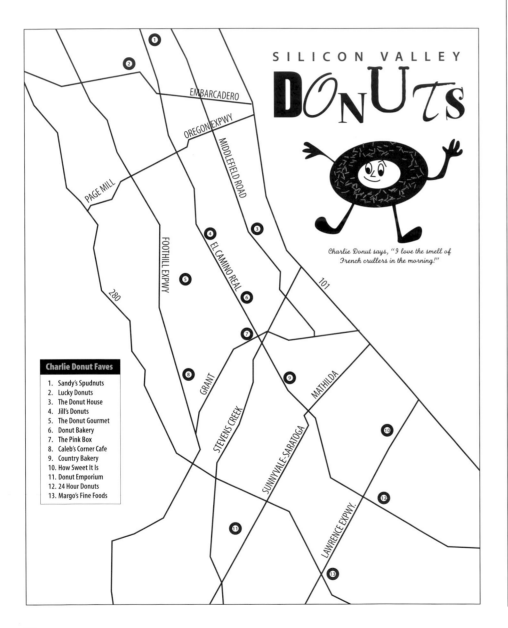

Use the new scatter brush in Illustrator as a symbol "library" for maps or other illustrations that require several copies of the same artwork. You could simply copy and paste several copies of a symbol, but the advantage to using the scatter brush is that you can make changes quickly and easily to all the symbols in the file at once. Or you can select and change individual symbol points without affecting all the others. This technique is a real time-saver, especially for mapmakers.

**1.** Create a symbol or graphic that you want to repeat several times on your map. Select the symbol artwork.

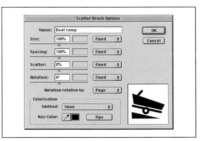

**2.** Choose Window > Show Brushes to display the Brushes palette. Click the New Brush button and select New Scatter Brush as the brush type. Give the brush a name and leave the settings as you see them here.

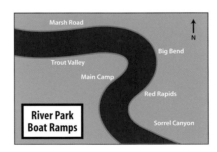

**3.** Open or create a background map.

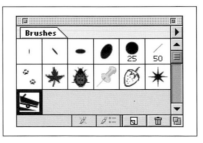

**4.** Choose the paintbrush from the toolbox and select the scatter brush you just created from the Brushes palette.

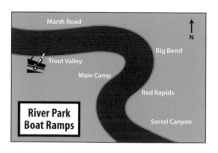

**5.** Click once—do not click and drag—to place one of the symbols on the map.

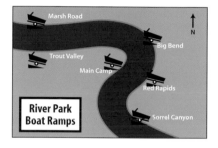

**6.** Continue clicking once in each place where you want the symbol to appear.

Depending on the symbol design, you may have some difficulty positioning the points accurately. This will be corrected in step 7.

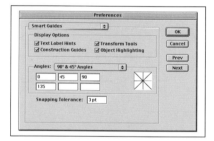

**7.** Choose File > Preferences > Smart Guides. Turn on Text Label Hints and Object Highlighting. Select the View menu and check to make sure Smart Guides is turned on. Click OK.

This will help you find the symbol points quickly if you want to select and reposition them.

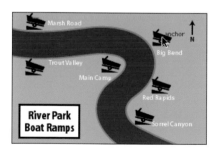

**8.** Choose the selection tool from the toolbox. Move the cursor over the symbol until the text label "anchor" appears. Then click on the anchor point and drag the symbol to the desired position. Reposition any other symbols if necessary. Save the file. If you want to change all of the symbols at once, continue with step 9.

**9.** Create the new or altered symbol.

In this example, I changed the color of the boat.

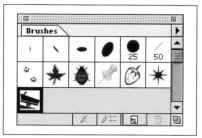

**10.** Select the new symbol artwork and Option/Alt-drag it into the Brushes palette. Position the cursor over the old symbol, and the old symbol will appear highlighted with a thick black box around it. Release the mouse button and the Option/Alt key.

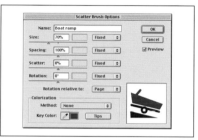

**11.** Make any other changes to the symbol scatter brush in the Scatter Brush Options dialog box. Click OK.

If you want the symbol to be scaled or rotated globally, you can do so now. In this example, I scaled the symbol by 70%.

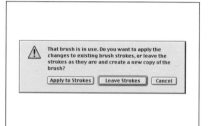

**12.** After you click OK in the Scatter Brush Options dialog box, you will get the message shown here. Click Apply to Strokes to change all the symbols in your map.

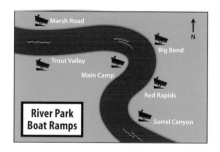

**13.** Save the file.

*Variation:* To change individual symbols without affecting the entire set, select the symbol point that you want to change. Click on the Options of Selected Object button in the Brushes palette and enter the changes.

In this example, I changed the stroke color of two of the points to purple and set the Colorization to Hue Shift.

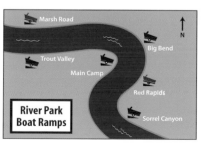

# 2 Painting

# Tissue-paper mosaics

*Adobe Illustrator 8.0 or later*

This technique uses a rasterized image to create tiles that can be overlapped for a tissue-paper collage look or can be organized with "grout" for a mosaic effect. Start with an illustration or a placed raster image and begin experimenting. I like to leave the original artwork on a layer in the background to fill in the holes that are left when I transform the tile artwork. But you could remove that layer for a confetti effect. For a stained glass effect, use black "grout."

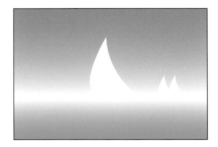

**1.** Create or open an illustration. If the artwork exists on several layers, choose Flatten artwork from the Layers palette pop-up menu to reduce the file to one layer.

If you want to retain the file with separate layers, choose File > Save As and save the flattened file with a different name.

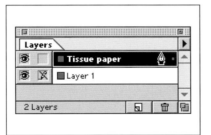

**2.** Option/Alt-drag the flattened layer onto the New Layer button to make a duplicate layer. Double-click the duplicate and name it *Tissue paper*. Lock the original layer.

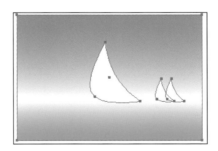

**3.** Choose Edit > Select All.

**4.** Choose Object > Rasterize to convert the selected illustration to a bitmap image. Turn on the Anti-Alias option and select either Medium or Screen Resolution. Click OK.

Since you will change this image to a mosaic of shapes, you don't need a high-resolution raster image.

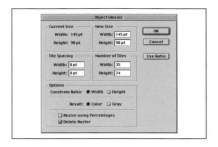

**5.** With the selection still active, choose Filter > Create > Object Mosaic to turn the raster image into a mosaic of squares. Select the Delete Raster option and enter the number of tiles you want for the Width. Click the Use Ratio button and the height will be calculated and entered for you. Click OK.

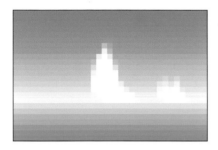

**6.** Choose View > Hide Edges so that the object remains selected and you can see the effect you will create in step 7.

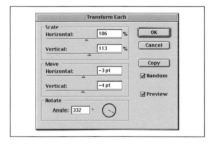

**7.** Choose Object > Transform > Transform Each to alter the tiles individually. Turn on the Preview option and increase the Scale values so the tiles overlap. Turn on the Random option and change the Move and Rotate values for a less regular effect. When you are happy with the preview, click OK.

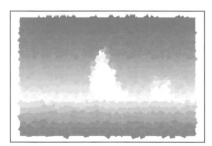

**8.** Choose View > Show Edges and then Edit > Deselect All to view the results.

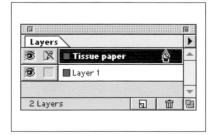

**9.** Lock the *Tissue paper* layer in the Layers palette and unlock the original layer.

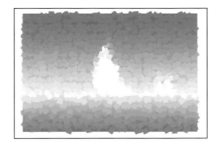

**10.** Select different paths on the original layer and alter their color slightly to set off the squares on the *Tissue paper* layer. Save the file.

In this example, I darkened the colors in the background gradient slightly.

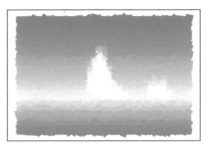

***Variation:*** Follow the first technique except use larger scale values in step 7. After step 7, while the tiles are still selected, display the Pathfinder palette and click the Soft Mix button.

This results in a transparent appearance where the tiles overlap.

### Tiles with Grout

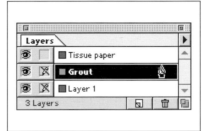

**1.** Follow steps 1 through 6 of the technique. Create a new layer and name it *Grout*. Move it just below the *Tissue paper* layer. Create a rectangle the same size as the raster image rectangle and fill it with a color that will be seen between the tiles in the next step. Lock the *Grout* layer.

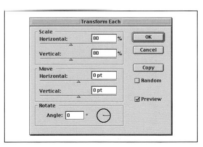

**2.** Continue with step 7 and reduce only the Horizontal and Vertical Scale percentages until you can see the *Grout* layer showing through the *Tissue paper* layer. For an even thickness of "grout," use the same value for both Horizontal and Vertical. Click OK.

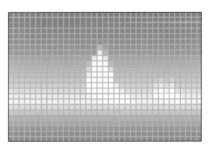

**3.** Save the file.

Because the "grout" is on a separate layer, you can easily select it and try as many different colors as you like.

# Painterly images

*Adobe Photoshop 5.0 or later*

Here's a way to turn your photographs into beautiful, textural digital paintings. Photoshop has many built-in filters that produce a "painterly" or "sketchy" texture. Here I separate the color from the texture to give you more control over the final effect. There are also several variations on the basic steps at the end of the technique. Just substitute the filter shown in the variation for the one used in step 8, and you'll get a very different result.

**1.** Open an RGB image. Much of the detail will be lost in this technique, so pick an image with a strong composition and vibrant colors.

The image should start in RGB mode because many of the filters used in this technique work only on RGB images.

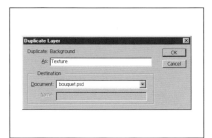

**2.** Option/Alt-drag the *Background* layer thumbnail onto the New Layer button to duplicate it. Name this layer *Texture*. This layer will define only the texture of the final image, not the color.

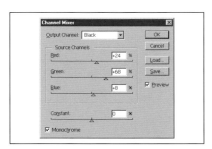

**3.** Choose Image > Adjust > Channel Mixer to remove the color. Select the Monochrome option and start out with the values in the illustration. Adjust for your image if necessary.

I used Channel Mixer because it has more flexibility than the Desaturate command.

**4.** Make a duplicate of the *Background* layer and name it *Color*. This layer will define the colors of your painting. Drag the *Color* layer above the *Texture* layer.

**5.** Set the mode for the *Color* layer to Color. Then hide the *Background* and *Texture* layers.

The Color mode retains the color from that layer but picks up the texture from the layers beneath it.

**6.** With the *Color* layer still selected, choose Filter > Blur > Smart Blur. In this example, I used a Radius of 60 and a Threshold of 73. Set the Quality to High and click OK.

Using Smart Blur this way simplifies the details in the image, giving it a cartoony or airbrushed look.

**7.** Select the *Texture* layer to make it active and visible.

**8.** Choose Filter > Artistic > Dry Brush. You will get different texture effects depending on the resolution of your image. Experiment with different values until you are happy with the texture. Click OK.

This example is 144 ppi, and I used a Brush Size of 3, a Brush Detail of 10, and a Texture of 2.

**9.** If you are satisfied with the effect, save or print the image. If you want to experiment with other textures and effects, try the following variations.

**Smart Blur variation**
Stop at step 6 and save the file.

**Colored Pencil variation**
Replace step 8 with: Choose Filter > Artistic > Colored Pencil.

**Settings:**
Pencil Width = 1
Stroke Pressure = 15
Paper Brightness = 50

**Fresco variation**

Replace step 8 with: Set the texture layer to 60% opacity and choose Filter > Artistic > Fresco.

**Settings:**

Brush Size = 8
Brush Detail = 2
Texture = 1

**Rough Pastels variation**

Replace step 8 with: Choose Filter > Artistic > Rough Pastels.

**Settings:**

Stroke Length = 10
Stroke Detail = 5
Texture = Canvas
Scaling = 69%
Relief = 34
Light Dir. = Bottom

**Poster Edges variation**

Replace step 8 with: Choose Filter > Artistic > Poster Edges.

**Settings:**

Edge Thickness = 0
Edge Intensity = 1
Posterization = 3

**Watercolor variation**

Replace step 8 with: Choose Filter > Artistic > Watercolor.

**Settings:**

Brush Detail = 14
Shadow Intensity = 0
Texture = 1

**Spatter variation**
Replace step 8 with:
Choose Filter >
Brush Strokes >
Spatter.

**Settings:**
Spray Radius = 3
Smoothness = 2

**Pointillize variation**
Replace step 8 with:
Choose Filter >
Pixelate > Pointillize.
Set background color
to 50% gray.

**Settings:**
Cell Size = 5

**Sprayed Strokes
variation**
Replace step 8 with:
choose Filter >
Brush Strokes >
Sprayed Strokes.

**Settings:**
Stroke Length = 16
Spray Radius = 14
Stroke Direction =
  Right Diagonal

**Texturizer variation**
Stop at step 6 and don't
create a texture layer.
Choose Filter > Texture >
Texturizer.

**Settings:**
Texture = Canvas
Scaling = 109%
Relief = 5
Light Dir. = Top Left

# Digital paintings

*Adobe Photoshop 5.0 or later*

In just a few simple steps, you can turn a run-of-the-mill snapshot or stock photo into a digital painting. Use the brushes available to you in the Photoshop Brushes palette or create your own to add texture and a more painterly feel. See page 34 for instructions on creating your own custom brushes. You may want to add texture by creating a "canvas" or "paper" background layer. If so, start with the Painting on "paper" procedure, and then continue with the digital painting procedure.

**1.** Open a new file. If the file has several layers, flatten them and choose File > Save As to save the file with a new name.

**2.** If your image has flat or dull colors, you might want to intensify them for the painting. Create an adjustment layer by Command/Ctrl-clicking the New Layer button. Choose Hue/Saturation. Move the Saturation slider to the right to intensify the colors in your image. Click OK.

**3.** Choose Merge Down from the Layers palette pop-up menu to combine the adjustment layer with the image layer. Choose View > Show History and click the New Snapshot button to create a new snapshot of the current state of your image. Click the left column of *Snapshot 1* to set it as the source for the history brush.

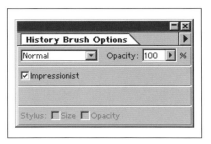

**4.** Select the history brush and turn on the Impressionist option in the History Brush Options palette.

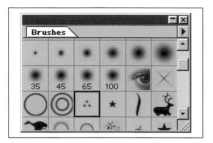

**5.** Choose either a brush from the Brushes palette or a custom brush that matches the texture of the subject matter.

To load a custom brush, select Load Brushes from the Brushes palette. Go to the Photoshop folder and open Goodies > Brushes & Patterns > Assorted Brushes.

**6.** Select your brush and begin painting the image. The impressionist tool samples the colors that are in the snapshot and allows you to move them around. It's as if the photo is made of wet paint and you are smearing it around with a brush.

**7.** You may want to zoom in to paint certain sections or objects in your image. Change the brushes or brush stroke direction based on the subject matter.

In this example, I tried to match the brush stroke direction to the texture of the trees.

**8.** Continue brushing the entire image until you are satisfied with the result. You may want to go back over certain areas with a smaller brush if some detail was lost that you want to recover.

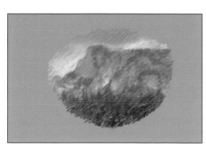

**Variation:** Introduce a "canvas color" to unify the image. After making the snapshot in step 3, fill the *Background* layer with a color. I usually pick a color from the image itself with the eyedropper tool. Then continue with step 4. As you are painting, let some of the background show through.

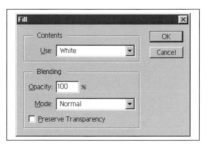

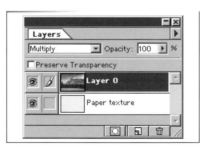

**Painting on "paper"**

**1.** Before you start the digital painting technique, create a new layer and name it *Paper texture* or *Canvas texture* depending on the texture you want to use.

**2.** Choose Edit > Fill and fill the *Paper texture* layer with 100% white.

**3.** Choose Filter > Texture > Texturizer. Select Load Texture from the Texture pull-down menu. Navigate to Adobe Photoshop 5.0 > Goodies > Textures on your hard drive. Select the Paper-Regular file and click OK.

Use the settings in the example or change them to suit your artwork.

**4.** Move the *Paper texture* layer below the layer you are going to paint on. If the painting layer is a *Background* layer, double-click on it to change it to a regular moveable, nameable layer. Set its layer mode to Multiply.

You should now see the paper texture through the image layer.

**5.** Perform steps 2 through 8 of the preceding technique.

# Natural media effects

*Adobe Photoshop 5.0 or later*

Even though I'm working with digitized images, I often want to create effects that look like I used a traditional drawing or painting tool. I create several tools before I start a project. Sometimes I use several different sizes of paint brushes. For example, I use a different brush size and texture to paint grass than I would use to paint a person's face. These techniques show you how to make and use two different tools — the paintbrush with bristles and the marker pen with transparent ink.

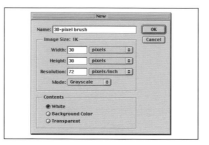

### Creating a bristle-brush effect

**1.** Create a new 30-pixel square grayscale file. Name the file after the brush size and click OK.

You will probably want several different sizes of paintbrushes, but in this example, I will make a 30-pixel brush.

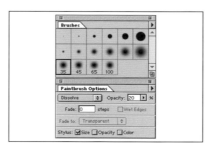

**2.** Select the paintbrush tool. From the Brushes palette, select a brush that is slightly larger in pixel size than the file you just created. Set the paintbrush mode to Dissolve and its Opacity to 20%.

If you're not sure how large a brush is, double-click it in the Brushes palette and you'll find the diameter in the Brush Options dialog box.

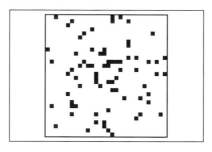

**3.** Enlarge the view of the brush file, and press the D key to return the foreground and background colors to black and white. Position the brush over the image area and click once. You should see a random scattering of black pixels.

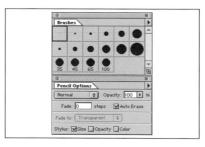

**4.** Select the pencil tool to edit the brush texture before continuing. Choose the 1-pixel brush and turn on the Auto Erase feature in the Pencil Options palette.

Auto Erase paints the background color over areas that contain the foreground color. This saves you from having to change back and forth between the eraser and pencil when editing.

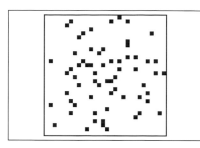

**5.** Click the pencil tool on the pixels you want to remove. If you want to add pixels, click in a white area. Try to keep the scattered pixels randomly spaced.

In this example, I removed a few of the pixels around the edges so that the brush has a rounder shape.

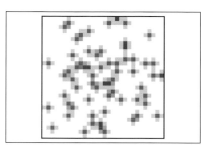

**6.** Choose Filter > Blur > Blur so that the brush strokes have a smoother, softer appearance.

For an even softer appearance, you can blur more than once.

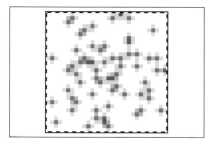

**7.** Choose Select > All, and then choose Define Brush from the pop-up menu on the Brushes palette.

The 30-pixel brush is now in your Brushes palette.

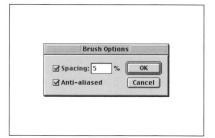

**8.** Double-click the brush that you just created in the Brushes palette. Change the Spacing amount to a smaller percentage.

Changing the spacing in the Brush Options palette creates those long striations in the brush strokes. I usually use a number between 1 and 10.

**9.** Choose the paintbrush and set the mode to Normal and begin painting.

This brush works very well with the Digital painting technique on page 32.

**Marker pen effect**

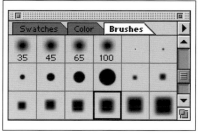

**1.** Select the paintbrush tool. Choose Load Brushes from the Brushes palette popup menu. Load the *Drop Shadow Brushes* file from the Brushes folder in the Goodies folder. Select one of the soft-edged square brushes.

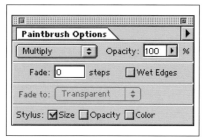

**2.** Set the painting mode to Multiply in the Paintbrush Options palette.

For a slightly different effect, turn on the Wet Edges option. The color will be lighter and the edges will be slightly darker.

**3.** Create a new layer and draw with your digital marker.

In this example, I used a pressure-sensitive tablet to vary the line width.

**4.** When you make a subsequent stroke that intersects a previously drawn mark, the intersection area will appear darker.

*Variation:* If you want the texture from other layers to show through the marker drawing, set the marker layer mode to Multiply. The color of the marks changes, but the texture shows through them, making the drawing look more like a real marker sketch.

# Color-tinted photographs

*Adobe Photoshop 5.0 or later*

In traditional photography, photographers rely on post-darkroom techniques to enhance black-and-white prints with color. Sepia-toning and iron-toning are two of these techniques; these processes tone the overall print with brown and blue, respectively. Hand-coloring with oil paints is another technique traditionally used to add color to photographs—sometimes to make a print look more realistic and sometimes for artistic effect.

A woman in the United States has a 1 in 8 lifetime risk of developing breast cancer

WHO ME?

October is Breast Cancer Awareness Month

### Color-tinting

**1.** Open the grayscale file you want to color tint. Convert the file to RGB. If you are starting with a color image, choose Image > Adjust > Desaturate to remove the existing color.

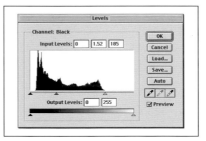

**2.** Command/Ctrl-click the New Layer button to create a new adjustment layer. Select Levels and move the histogram highlight and midtone sliders to the left.

The goal here is to lighten the image so that you can clearly see the color-tinting.

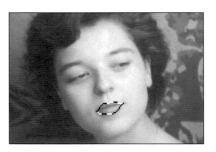

**3.** Select the area or shape to tint.

This selection has a feather value of 1 because the lips are not hard-edged.

**4.** Create a new layer and set its mode to Color.

Use a different layer for each different color or shape so that editing and changing colors are easy.

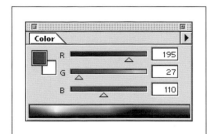

**5.** Choose a color to fill the selection.

Don't worry if the color seems too intense or saturated. Adjust the layer's opacity if it's too dark.

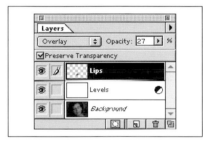

**6.** Make sure that the selection is still active and that the proper layer is targeted. Fill the selection with the foreground color.

If you want objects at different opacities on the same layer, choose Edit > Fill and change the opacity as you fill each selection.

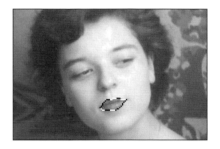

**7.** Adjust the opacity on the layer if desired. To change colors quickly, turn on the Preserve Transparency option. Choose a new color and fill the layer without selecting anything.

In this example, only the lip area will be filled with a new color.

**8.** Repeat steps 3 through 7 for each area that needs tinting.

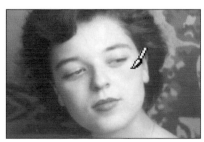

*Variation:* You can use a painting tool to paint tints on the color layer instead of filling with color in step 6. However, you may still want to make selections to protect certain areas from the color.

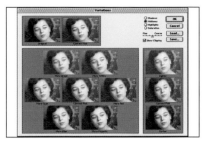

### Sepia- and iron-toning

**1.** To make a sepia-tone photograph, follow the preceding steps 1 and 2. Choose Image > Adjust > Variations. Set the slider to Fine if you want to make subtle color changes.

Clicking on the variations will gradually change the overall color of the image.

**2.** Set the slider two notches above Fine and add Red and Yellow a couple of times. Then add Blue once to get a sepia tone.

To simulate iron-toning, follow these steps but click the Blue, Cyan, and Green variations.

### Selective Color Recovery

**1.** Open an RGB file and create a snapshot in the History palette. Follow steps 1 and 2 of the color-tinting procedure.

**2.** Make a new snapshot of the grayscale version. Set the source for the history brush to the color snapshot you took in step 1.

**3.** Select the history brush and paint in the areas that you want to return to full color.

Or if you prefer, make selections and choose Edit > Fill. Then choose History in the Contents pop-up menu. If you make an error or paint in too much color, set the history brush source to the grayscale snapshot and repair the image.

# Outlined images

*Adobe Photoshop 5.0 or later*

You can turn a flat or dull photograph into a graphic illustration with this technique. Start with an image that has edges that you want to emphasize. The best images for this technique are simple without a lot of contrasty texture. You'll end up with a Color layer that has a softened, "airbrushed" look to it and an Outline layer that overlays the Color layer. There are a couple of variations on the types of outlines you can make. Try each of them with your image to see which looks best.

**1.** Open an image that you want to outline. Use an image of at least 300 dpi because the outline edges look better. Images that have interesting, clearly defined edges work best.

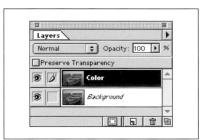

**2.** Option/Alt-drag the layer you want to outline onto the New Layer icon to make a duplicate. Name the layer *Color*.

In this example, I applied the effect to the *Background* layer.

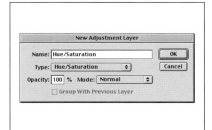

**3.** To intensify the colors, create an adjustment layer by Command/Ctrl-clicking on the New Layer button in the Layers palette. Choose Hue/Saturation as the Type. Click OK.

To make the image look more like an illustration, try to create a more surreal color scheme.

**4.** Adjust the Hue, Saturation, or Lightness to make your image more dramatic.

I'm not recommending specific values here because each image will require a different adjustment. You can change an adjustment layer at any time, so you'll be able to make more color changes later, if necessary.

**5.** Select the *Color* layer and choose Filter > Blur > Smart Blur. Set the Quality to High and the Mode to Normal. Start with the Radius and Threshold values shown here, and then adjust them for your image. The goal is to smooth out the inside of the shapes while retaining crisp edges. Click OK.

**6.** Evaluate the resulting *Color* layer. It should be missing much of its original texture. The shapes should be simplified and should have well-defined edges. If you are not satisfied with the result, undo and try step 5 again with different values.

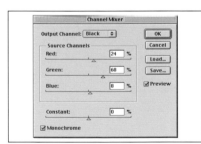

**7.** Option/Alt-drag the *Color* layer onto the New Layer button to duplicate it. Name this layer *Outline*.

**8.** Choose Image > Adjust > Channel Mixer to remove the color from the image. Select Monochrome and use the settings shown in the example. Adjust the values if necessary to retain the edge detail in your image. Click OK.

I removed the color before creating the outline so that I ended up with black edges in step 9.

**9.** Create the outlines by choosing Filter > Stylize > Find Edges.

**10.** Set the *Outline* layer mode to Darken. If you are satisfied with the result, stop here. If the image still needs some finessing, continue with step 11.

Darken applies only the dark edges to the image. The white areas are ignored.

**11.** If the outlines are too weak or if they are too thick, correct them with another adjustment layer. Command/Ctrl-click on the New Layer button. Select Brightness/Contrast and turn on the Group With Previous Layer option.

**12.** Adjust the Brightness/Contrast values until you are satisfied with the outlines. Click OK.

***Variation 1:*** If you want less black and more color in your outlines, try skipping step 8. Then set the *Outline* layer mode to Multiply.

***Variation 2:*** If you want a bitmap-quality outline, use the Smart Blur filter instead of the Find Edges filter in step 9. Choose the Edge Only mode. Then choose Image > Adjust > Invert to invert the *Outline* layer and continue with step 10.

# Stippling

*Adobe Photoshop 5.0 or later*
*Adobe Illustrator 8.0 or later (optional)*

I like the rich textural look of different colors spatter-painted or airbrushed on top of each other. Using several different colors for shadows instead of just black creates a richer effect. You can add dimension and character to your type or graphics using textured gradations. First build a different layer for each color you want to spatter onto your image. Then add a layer mask and texturize it. You'll end up with a multi-layered file that is very versatile. You can experiment with different colors, layer modes, and textures as you lay one colored texture on top of another.

**1.** Create a basic design with flat shapes of color. Make a separate layer for each different colored object.

If you use graphics created in Illustrator, export them in Photoshop 5 format. Choose the Write Layers option and open the file in Photoshop.

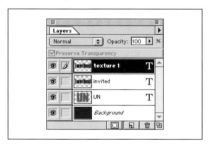

**2.** Select the layer of the first graphic you want to texturize. Make a copy of that layer by Option/ Alt-dragging it onto the New Layer button in the Layers palette. Name the new layer *Texture 1*. Turn on the Preserve Transparency option.

If the layer is a type layer, Preserve Transparency will be turned on automatically.

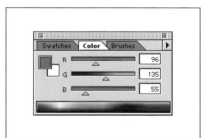

**3.** Choose a color that you want to "stipple" onto the base color of the original shape.

**4.** Fill the *Texture 1* layer with the foreground color. Don't worry about the color covering up the original. The stipple texture will be applied in the next few steps.

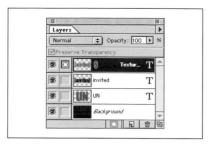

5. Option/Alt-click the New Layer Mask button to add a layer mask to the *Texture 1* layer. Pressing the Option/Alt key fills the layer mask with black, which blocks out the new color until you change it.

6. With the layer mask still selected, choose Filter > Noise > Add Noise. Turn on the Preview option so you can see the effect on your image. When you have the amount of color and texture that looks good with your graphic, click OK.

7. Evaluate the result. If you don't want to add any more stipple colors to this graphic, repeat steps 2 through 7 for any other layers in your file that need stippling. For multi-color stippling, continue with step 8.

You might be satisfied with adding just one color, but I usually mix at least two or three colors together for a richer effect.

8. Repeat steps 2 through 5 and name the new layer *Texture 2*.

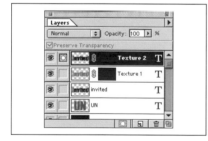

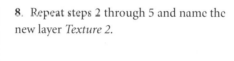

9. Reapply the Add Noise filter just as you did in step 6, but this time use a different amount. In this example, I wanted more purple dots than green, so I increased the Noise amount. Repeat steps 8 and 9 for as many colors as you want to add. Stop and save the file or continue with step 10 if you want to create a stippled gradation.

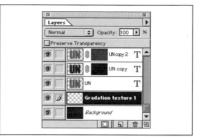

**Stippled gradations**

10. Make a new layer and position it directly over the layer you want to stipple. Name the layer *Gradation texture 1*.

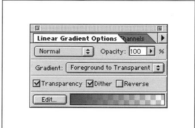

11. Change the foreground color to the color you want to use for the stippled gradation. Double-click the gradient tool to display the Linear Gradient Options palette. Change the Gradient type to Foreground to Transparent.

12. Apply a gradient to the *Gradation texture 1* layer with the gradient tool.

Don't worry if there is too much color at this point. You can control the amount of color added by how much noise you use in the next step.

13. Repeat steps 5 and 6 to add the layer mask with the stipple texture.

14. Add the stipple texture to the remaining elements in your design.

Shadows have color and texture, too, so don't forget to stipple the shaded areas with several colors instead of just black.

# Neon graphics

*Adobe Photoshop 5.0 or later*
*Adobe Illustrator 8.0 or later (optional)*

Making graphics glow in Photoshop is easy, but making digital neon is a different matter. Real neon signs and graphics are made from colored tubes filled with gas. The tubes are the same width and are wrapped and twisted to make shapes and letterforms. To make digital neon, I use paths created in either Illustrator or Photoshop. Then I create a tubal gradation by layering progressively smaller stroked paths on top of each other. The first stroke defines the outer glow, the inner strokes define the basic color, and the final stroke creates the bright "hot" inner glow of our digital neon "gas."

**1.** Design the neon base artwork using the pen tool in either Illustrator or Photoshop. Leave plenty of space between the paths so that you can increase the line thickness.

The advantage to using Illustrator is that you can experiment with the thickness and colors of the lines.

**2.** Create a background in Photoshop that is black or contains very dark tones to set off the "neon" artwork. Make a new layer and call it *Neon*.

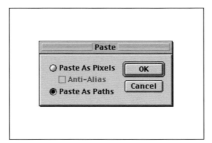

**3.** If you created your artwork in Photoshop, skip to step 5. If you created your artwork in Illustrator, copy it and paste it into your Photoshop file. Select the Paste As Paths option.

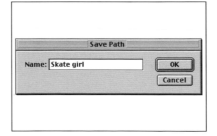

**4.** Double-click on the Work Path name in the Paths palette and save the path.

Note: All paths can be on the same path name.

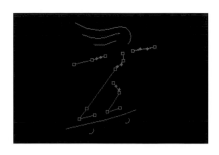

**5.** Select the first path or paths that share the same color.

You can press the Command/Ctrl key in any tool, and the cursor will change to the arrow tool when it's positioned over a path.

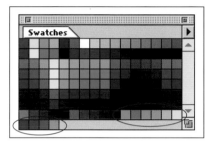

**6.** Create a set of three or four colors for the neon glow. You'll want a bright glow color and at least two midtone colors. Add them to your Swatches Palette for later use.

Notice that I added a green set of three, a yellow set of three, and a red set of four colors.

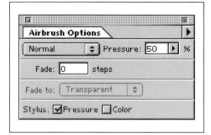

**7.** Double-click the airbrush tool in the toolbox and set the mode to Normal and the Pressure to 50%.

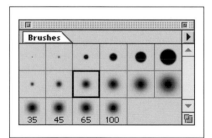

**8.** Select a large soft-edged brush from the Brushes palette.

This will be the width of the outer glow of the neon "tube." All the other brushes used will be smaller than this one.

**9.** Choose the *Neon* layer and select the second brightest color from the swatches you saved in step 6. With the path(s) still selected, choose Stroke Subpaths from the Paths palette. It will show you that the airbrush is the selected tool. Click OK.

A shortcut for stroking an active path with the current tool is to press the Enter key.

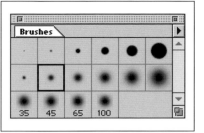

**10.** Choose a smaller soft brush. Select one of the midtone colors from the swatches you created.

If you want the flexibility to adjust the colors later, make a different layer for each new stroke color. To change the colors easily, turn on the Preserve Transparency option for those layers before you fill with a new color.

**11.** Stroke the path with the new color and brush the same way you did in step 9.

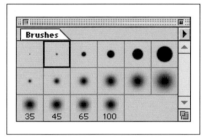

**12.** Select a smaller brush than you did in step 10. Select the brightest color in your swatch set.

For a more defined "tube highlight," choose a much smaller brush than the last one used. If you want a softer gradation of color, always use the next smaller brush size.

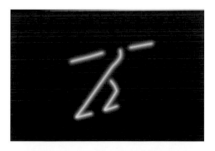

**13.** Stroke the path with the new color and brush the same way you did in step 9. Deselect the path(s) for a better preview.

**14.** Repeat steps 8 through 13 for each different color path or paths.

In this example, I used four different colors and brushes for the red skateboard.

# Cast shadows

*Adobe Photoshop 5.0 or later*

One of the toughest types of images to make is a really good composite. There are a few tricks, however, for creating the illusion that different images from different photos fit together. One trick is to make realistic cast shadows. This technique takes you through the basic steps of how to place an object into a background, adjust its color, and create a cast shadow. You may need to deviate from the instructions for your images. Try different colors for the shadow, or play with different transformation amounts in step 8. If you don't get the gradation angle correct in step 13, keep trying until you're happy with it.

**1.** Open the background for your composite image.

Notice the color of the light and the direction of the shadows.

**2.** Open another file and select the object you want to bring into the background image.

Pay attention to the light color and shadow direction. In this example, the light is coming from the opposite direction and is much cooler than in my background image. These problems will be corrected later.

**3.** Use the move tool to drag the object onto the background. A new layer will be created. Name this layer *Object*. Position the object and scale if necessary.

Notice that the elephant seems to float in the air without a cast shadow.

**4.** Option/Alt-drag the *Object* layer thumbnail onto the New Layer button to create a duplicate. Name this layer *Shadow*. Turn on the Preserve Transparency option for the *Shadow* layer.

**5.** Use the eyedropper tool to select a shadow color from the shadows in the background image. If no shadows exist, create a dark color in the Color palette.

**6.** Fill the *Shadow* layer with the foreground color.

Because the Preserve Transparency option is turned on, only the areas on the layer that contain pixels will be filled.

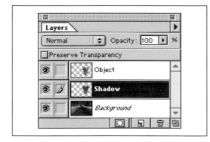

**7.** Move the *Shadow* layer down in the Layers palette so that it is below the *Object* layer. Turn off the Preserve Transparency option for the *Shadow* layer.

**8.** Choose Edit > Transform > Distort. Grab one corner of the shadow to pull it in the direction you want it to fall. Continue to transform the shadow until its shape and angle are consistent with the light angle and direction. Make sure the base of the shadow is touching the object that "casts" it. Press Enter to finish the transformation.

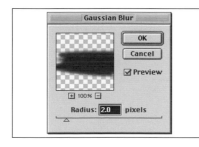

**9.** Choose Filter > Blur > Gaussian Blur. Turn on the Preview option so you can decide which Radius amount works for your image. When it looks right, click OK.

The Radius amount depends on resolution and existing shadows. Try to match the edge softness of other shadows in the background.

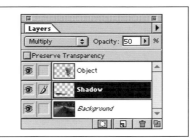

**10.** Set the *Shadow* layer mode to Multiply and adjust the Opacity.

The Multiply mode darkens the layers underneath but still allows the texture of the lower layers to show through.

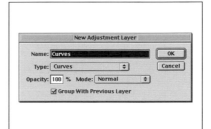

**11.** Select the *Object* layer in the Layers palette. Command/Ctrl-click on the New Layer button to create a new adjustment layer. Select the Group With Previous Layer option. Choose either Levels or Curves as the type.

This adjustment layer will alter the color cast of the object.

**12.** Turn on the Preview option in the Levels or Curves dialog. Adjust the shadows and highlights so that the image appears to naturally fit into the background's lighting.

In this example, I adjusted the Blue curve so that the image would seem warmer and its highlights would look more yellow.

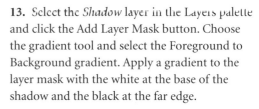

**13.** Select the *Shadow* layer in the Layers palette and click the Add Layer Mask button. Choose the gradient tool and select the Foreground to Background gradient. Apply a gradient to the layer mask with the white at the base of the shadow and the black at the far edge.

The shadow will fade in the direction of the gradient vector.

**14.** Use the Dodge/Burn tool to correct other small lighting problems.

In this example, I darkened the left side of the elephant a bit. I also darkened its feet slightly.

# Transparent shadows

*Adobe Illustrator 8.0 or later*

Designers and illustrators commonly need semitransparent shapes for shadows that overlap other objects in their drawings. Although Illustrator can't create true transparent objects, you can easily use it to simulate transparency. The Flat color shadow method creates a semitransparent shadow using solid colors and the Hard Mix command in the Pathfinder palette. The Gradient shadow method creates a more subtle effect using gradient fills and the gradient fill tool.

**Flat color shadow**

**1.** Make sure that the artwork is sized, painted, and positioned as you want it. If any type falls within the shadow area, select the type and choose Type > Create Outlines. If a stroked object falls in the shadow area, select the object and choose Object > Path > Outline Path.

**2.** Option/Alt-click on the New Layer button in the Layers palette to create a new layer. Name it *Shadow*. Move it so it is directly beneath the layer of the object that will be casting the shadow.

**3.** Create the shadow shape and fill it with a tint of black. Arrange it so that the shadow is in front of the objects it will shade and behind the object casting it.

In this example, I used a 25% black fill.

**4.** Lock the *Shadow* layer to protect it while you edit the surrounding shapes. Choose File > Preferences > Smart Guides and turn on Object Highlighting to assist you in finding hidden paths. Select the shape or shapes that fall within the shadow. If any two shapes overlap beneath the shadow, click the Divide button on the Pathfinder palette to separate the colors.

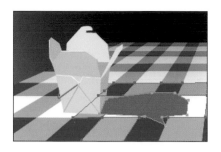

**5.** Select all the shapes that are overlapped by the shadow. Unlock the *Shadow* layer. Press the Shift key and select the shadow shape as well.

**6.** Click the Hard Mix button on the Pathfinder palette. Deselect and save the file.

The Hard Mix command brings the objects up to the layer of the topmost object, which is the *Shadow* layer.

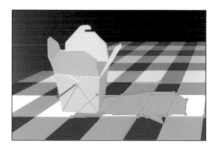

**Gradient shadow**

**1.** Follow steps 1 through 3 of the Flat shadow technique. Select the shadow and all the shapes behind it. Click the Divide button on the Pathfinder palette.

**2.** Choose Window > Show Gradient to display the Gradient palette. Deselect any selected artwork. Choose the *Black, White* linear gradient from the default set in the Color palette. Select the leftmost gradient slider, which is set to white.

**3.** Select the eyedropper tool from the toolbox. Position it over one of the shapes that falls beneath the shadow. Shift-click on the color to apply the fill color to the selected gradient slider.

**4.** Select the shape or shapes that were originally filled with the color you just added to the gradient.

**5.** Fill the selected shapes with the new gradient.

The gradient won't look correct inside these shapes yet. You will adjust the gradient angle in step 8.

**6.** Repeat steps 3 through 5 for each different colored object that falls within the shadow area. For white areas, use the *Black, White* gradient.

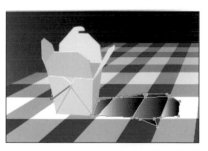

**7.** Select all the gradient-filled shapes that create the shadow shape.

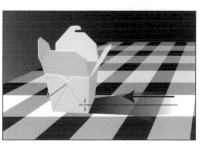

**8.** Choose View > Hide Edges so you can see the gradients without the selection edges. Select the gradient tool from the toolbox and drag to define the angle and length of the gradients.

Remember that the lighter color will be placed where you first click, and the black will be where you release the mouse button. Deselect and save.

# Gradients on a path

*Adobe Illustrator 8.0 or later*

Need to create neon, rainbows, tubes, or pipes? Then this is the technique to use. First create an art brush from a gradient. (Create your own gradient or use one of the many gradients installed in your Gradient Libraries folder.) Then apply it to a path. One advantage to using the art brush gradient is that you can quickly and easily change its color. Another is that if you edit the path, the gradient automatically reflows along the new path. If you want to create a three-dimensional effect on shapes with corners or sharp bends, use Variation 2 and make your art brush into a pattern brush with corners.

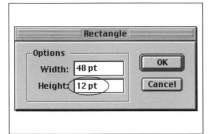

**1.** Select the rectangle tool. Position the cursor in a blank area of the file and click once. Enter the Width and Height amounts. The Width amount should be a few times larger than the Height. The Height amount should be the thickness that you want your path gradient to be.

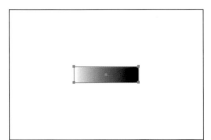

**2.** Fill the rectangle with the *Black, White* gradient, which is one of the default gradients found in the Swatches palette. Stroke the rectangle with None.

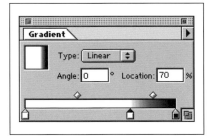

**3.** Choose Window > Show Gradient to display the Gradient palette. The *Black, White* gradient will appear in the palette. Click below the gradient bar to add a new color. Select white in the Color palette to fill the square with white. Position the new color square at the 70% location. If this is difficult, type in the value and press Enter.

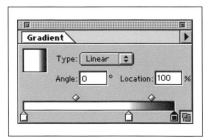

**4.** Select the far right color square on the gradient bar. Select 80% black in the Color palette.

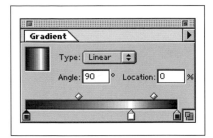

**5.** Select the leftmost color square on the gradient bar. Select 80% black in the Color palette. Change the angle to 90°.

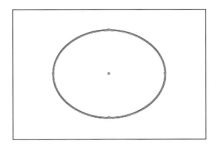

**10.** Create a path to which you can apply the gradient art brush. Stroke it with the color that you want to be the main color of the tube gradient. Fill it with None if you want only the tube gradient to show.

Art brushes that have Colorization methods of Tints, Tints and Shades, or Hue Shift will use the color of a path's stroke, not its fill.

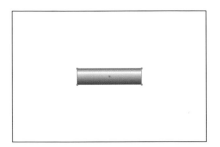

**6.** Evaluate the results. You should have a grayscale version of the tubular gradation you will eventually apply to a path. If you need to do any resizing or color editing, do it now.

You'll be converting the gradient to shapes in order to create an art brush in step 9.

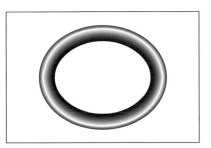

**11.** With the path still selected, click on the gradient art brush you just created in the Brushes palette. Save the file.

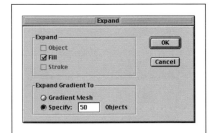

**7.** Choose Object > Expand to change the gradient into a series of shapes. The number of Objects you specify will depend on the height of the rectangle.

In this example, I specified 50 Objects for a 12-point thick tube. You may need to experiment with this value to create the smoothest blend.

*Variation 1:* Replace steps 3 through 6 with the following. Fill the rectangle with the *Rainbow* gradient from the default set in the Swatches palette and continue with step 7.

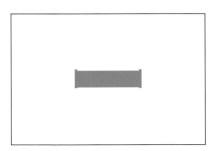

**8.** Choose Window > Show Pathfinder to display the Pathfinder palette. With the expanded gradient still selected, click the Crop button in the Pathfinder palette.

Once the gradient is expanded, the original rectangle becomes a mask for the blended shapes. Crop trims the shapes and removes the mask. Art brushes cannot contain masks.

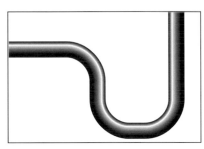

*Variation 2:* Use your gradient art brush artwork to create tiles for a pattern brush. Use the technique on page 4 to create a side tile and inner and outer corner tiles. Apply the new pattern brush to a path with corners.

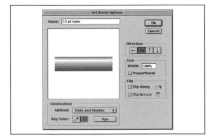

**9.** Use the popup menu on the Brushes palette to make sure Show Art Brushes is selected. Click the New Brush button and select Art Brush as the type. Name the new brush and select Tints and Shades as the Colorization method. Click OK.

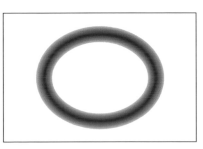

*Variation 3:* Replace the color squares in the gradient in steps 3 through 5 with the following: Set the 0% and 100% locations to 100% white. Set the 70% location to 50% black and move it to the 50% location, then continue with step 6.

# 3 Patterns and textures

# Simple patterns

*Adobe Illustrator 8.0 or later*

The simplest way to construct a pattern tile is to draw any graphic object and surround it with a rectangle placed in the background. This procedure describes how to take it a step further and create dense patterns that tile perfectly by positioning copies of the graphic in each corner of the background rectangle. Once you've created the basic pattern swatch, you can transform it with any of the transformation tools. You can also make copies of the swatch and create different color ways for design experimentation.

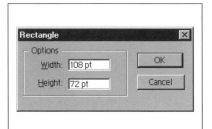

**1.** Select the rectangle tool and create a rectangle the size you want your pattern tile. For the most efficient printing and previewing, try to keep it between 1-2 inches square.

Note: Do not use the rounded rectangle tool for this step. The rectangle must have square corners.

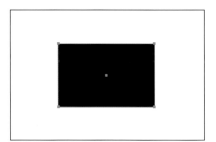

**2.** Fill the rectangle with the color that will be the background color of your pattern. If you want the pattern to have a transparent background, fill and stroke it with None. If you want a solid background, stroke it with None.

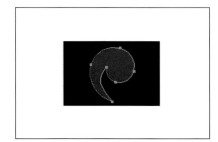

**3.** Create or copy and paste the artwork you want to use as a repeating element in your pattern. Check the View menu to be sure Snap to Point and Smart Guides are turned on.

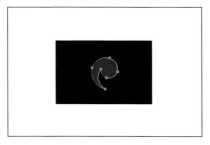

**4.** If the element is the correct size for the pattern, skip this step. If it needs to be scaled, select the scale tool from the toolbox and scale the element.

The element must be small enough that one can fit in the center and in each of the four corners without touching one another.

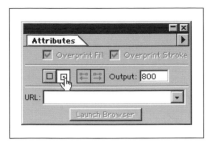

**5.** Choose View > Show Attributes to display the Attributes palette. With the object selected, click the Show Center button to display the center point of the element.

**6.** Use the selection tool and grab the element by the center point. Drag it until it snaps to the upper-left corner point of the rectangle. Don't release the mouse until you see the cursor turn to a white arrowhead, indicating the points have snapped.

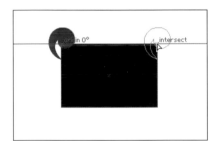

**7.** Grab the element again by its center point. Begin to drag it, and then press the Shift and Option/Alt keys to constrain and copy it. Drag until it snaps to the upper-right corner point of the rectangle. Don't release the mouse until you see the cursor turn to a white arrowhead, and the intersect hint appears. Release the mouse button and then the Shift and Option/Alt keys.

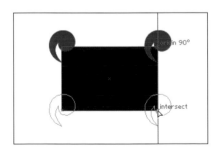

**8.** Select both top elements. Grab the right element by its center point. Begin to drag it down, and then press the Shift and Option/Alt keys. Drag until it snaps to the lower-right corner point of the rectangle. Release the mouse button and then the Shift and Option/Alt keys.

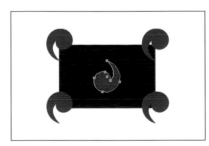

**9.** Place any additional graphics you want within the rectangle. Make sure that these elements don't overlap the rectangle edges. If they do, the pattern won't tile correctly.

In this example, I added a rotated version of my element and placed its center point over the center point of the rectangle.

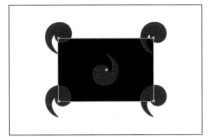

**10.** If you are already using a transparent rectangle as a background, skip to step 12. If your rectangle is stroked or filled, select the rectangle. Choose Edit > Copy and, while the rectangle is still selected, choose Edit > Paste in Back. Do NOT deselect yet.

It won't look like it, but you now have two rectangles stacked on top of each other.

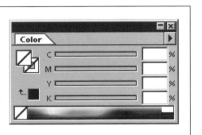

**11.** With the backmost rectangle still selected, paint it with a stroke and fill of None.

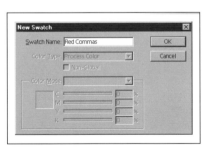

**12.** Select the rectangles and the elements.

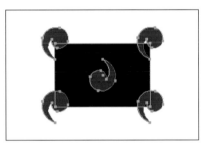

**13.** Choose Edit > Define Pattern. Give your pattern a name and click OK. The new pattern swatch will appear in the Swatches palette.

**14.** Create a shape, and then click on the swatch in the Swatches palette to fill the shape with your new pattern.

# Texture patterns

*Adobe Illustrator 8.0 or later*

You can create the effect of an uneven texture by constructing a pattern that appears irregular when it tiles. To achieve this effect, the edges of the pattern tile must match up perfectly so that the tiling results in one continuous texture. These textures take time to finesse, so once you've got a tile that works, try making different versions of it with different colors and stroke weights. If you need something quick, try starting with some premade tiles by loading the Pattern samples libraries that came with your program. Then customize the tile for your own needs.

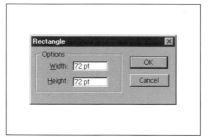

**1.** Select the rectangle tool and create a rectangle the size you want your pattern tile.

For the most efficient printing and previewing, try to keep it between 1-2 inches square.

Note: Do not use the rounded rectangle tool for this step. The rectangle must have square corners.

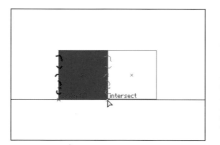

**2.** Fill the square with the color that will be the background color of your pattern. If you want the pattern to have a transparent background, fill and stroke it with None. Begin drawing the texture with just the shapes or lines that intersect the left side of the square. Select the square and the texture.

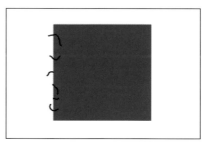

**3.** Check the View menu to be sure Snap to Point and Smart Guides are turned on. Position the cursor on the lower-left corner of the square. Begin dragging the artwork to the right; then press the Shift and Option/Alt keys to constrain and leave a copy. When the cursor snaps to the lower-right corner point, release the mouse button and then the Shift and Option/Alt keys.

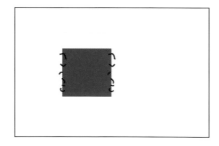

**4.** Select the right square and delete it.

**5.** Continue drawing your texture by adding shapes or lines that intersect only the top of the square. When you have finished, select the rectangle and the top texture only.

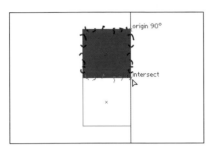

**6.** Position the cursor on the upper-right corner of the square. Begin dragging the artwork down; then press the Shift and Option/Alt keys to constrain and leave a copy. When the cursor snaps to the lower-right corner point, release the mouse button and then the Shift and Option/Alt keys.

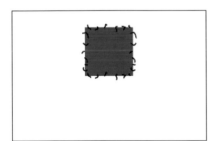

**7.** Select the lower square and delete it.

**8.** Fill in the middle of the square with your texture. Be careful not to intersect any of the square's edges or corners.

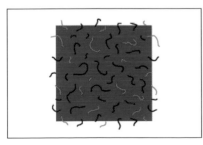

**9.** For a more varied texture, try using more than one color for the texture elements. If you repaint any edge pieces, be sure to paint the corresponding edge piece on the opposite side the same way.

Subtle color differences enhance the illusion that this is a texture instead of a repeating pattern.

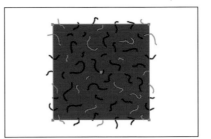

**10.** If you are already using a transparent square as a background, skip to step 12. If your square is stroked or filled, select the square. Choose Edit > Copy and while the square is still selected, choose Edit > Paste in Back. DO NOT deselect yet.

You now have two squares stacked on top of each other. One becomes a bounding box.

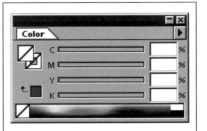

**11.** With the backmost square still selected, paint it with a stroke and fill of None.

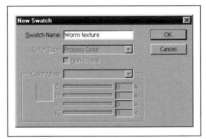

**12.** Select the square and the texture elements. Choose Edit > Define Pattern. Give your pattern a name and click OK. The new pattern swatch will appear in the Swatches palette.

**13.** Create a large rectangle and select the pattern from the Swatches palette to fill it with the new pattern. Zoom out and look for places in the texture that create an obvious repeating pattern. If necessary, return to the pattern tile and adjust the artwork to smooth out obvious holes or clumps. The goal is to get a smooth, even texture with no obvious repetition.

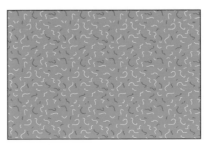

*Variation:* Select the pattern tile from step 10 and choose Filter > Colors > Invert Colors. Then continue with step 11.

Once you've got a texture that works, create different color versions so you can use it several times instead of just once.

# Seamless patterns

*Adobe Photoshop 5.0 or later*

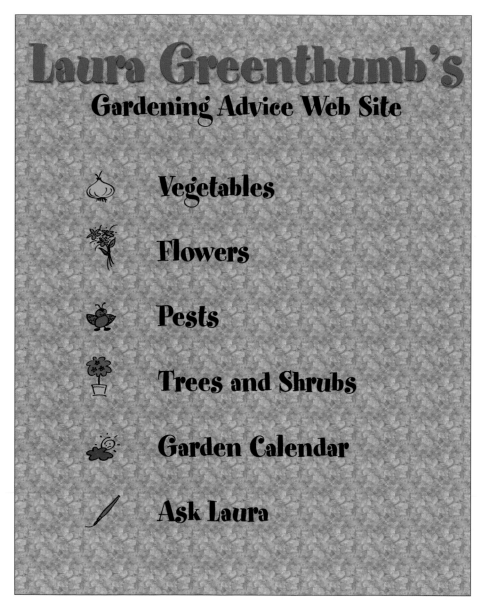

To make a pattern in Photoshop, you simply select an area using the rectangle marquee tool and then choose Edit > Define Pattern. Almost always, however, filling an area with this pattern will leave telltale tiling seams, or grids. For a pattern to tile seamlessly, the edges of the pattern tiles must align exactly to create a continuous image. This technique shows how to create a pattern tile with edges that won't be visible when the tile repeats. The types of images that work best with this technique have soft, blurry backgrounds or plenty of texture. Images with strong lines are difficult because it's hard to match up the lines at the proper angle.

**1.** Open the image that contains the area you want to use for a pattern tile.

Images with plain or textured backgrounds make the best seamless patterns because their tile lines are easier to smooth away. Avoid images that bleed off the edge of the tile and images with gradations; they're difficult to touch up.

**2.** Select the crop tool from the toolbox and crop the image to the size and area you want the pattern tile to be.

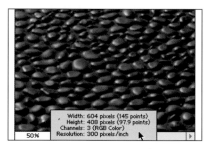

**3.** Check the size of the file by holding down Option/Alt and selecting the size box in the lower-left corner of the window or menu bar. Make a note of the width and height pixel values for later use.

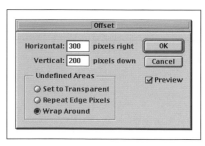

**4.** Choose Filter > Other > Offset. Select the Wrap Around option; for the horizontal and vertical values, enter approximately half the value of the width and height you noted in step 3.

This filter basically slices up your image and moves it horizontally and vertically. It is helpful to do this so you can see how the edges of the pattern tiles will meet. Click OK.

**5.** Examine the result.

The Offset filter splits the image into four sections. Notice that the left half of the image completes the right half, and the top half of the image completes the bottom half. The seams you see would be visible had you taken the cropped image from step 2 and used it as a pattern tile.

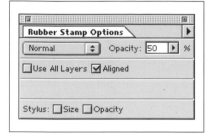

**6.** Double-click the rubber stamp tool in the toolbox to select it and display the Rubber Stamp Options palette. Choose the Aligned option and set the Opacity to approximately 50%.

The Opacity setting will depend on the texture you are cloning and the brush you use. Start with 50% and increase or decrease as needed.

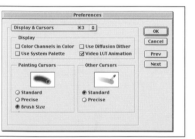

**7.** Choose File > Preferences > Display & Cursors. Select the Brush Size option for Painting Cursors.

Using a Brush Size cursor is a much more accurate and predictable way to clone images because you can see where the outer edge of the brush is.

**8.** Select a brush that is similar in size and softness to the object you will be cloning. Option/Alt-click to sample an image or texture area that you want to clone over the seam.

In this example, I chose a soft-edged brush because the image is slightly soft, not sharp.

**9.** Use the rubber stamp tool to eliminate the center seams between the four sections of the image. Try to clone using multiple, short brush strokes so that the stroke itself is not visible.

The goal is to try to blend the backgrounds of each rectangle together and to remove other elements that you don't want to repeat.

**10.** Continue sampling and cloning until you have covered the seams.

Be prepared to spend some time on this step. Depending on the image, it can take quite a while to do a good job covering up the seams.

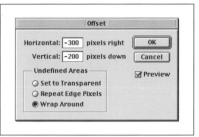

**11.** Choose Filter > Other > Offset to check your work. Add a minus before each of the pixel values to reverse the offset effect. Click OK.

**12.** Choose Select > All; then choose Edit > Define Pattern.

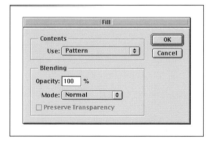

**13.** Create a new file to use as a pattern fill test. Make sure that the file is several times larger than the pattern tile. Select a large area (or the entire file) and choose Edit > Fill. From the Use pop-up menu, choose Pattern. Click OK.

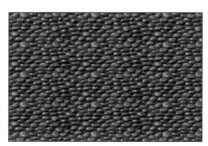

**14.** Evaluate the overall look of the pattern and identify any problem areas. If you like the effect, save the pattern tile file. If you want to touch up the tile, repeat steps 4 through 13.

# Illustrator pattern tiles in Photoshop

*Adobe Photoshop 5.0 or later*
*Adobe Illustrator 8.0 or later*

Illustrator comes with several libraries full of hundreds of pattern tiles that can be used in Photoshop. You can find a small number of the pattern tiles in the Patterns folder in the Photoshop application folder. This technique describes how to use these Illustrator pattern tiles or pattern tiles you've created using the technique on pages 54 and 56, in Photoshop. You'll use Illustrator to perfect the artwork so that it tiles seamlessly. Then you'll apply the pattern to your image in Photoshop and use layer modes and effects to enhance it.

**1.** Create a new Illustrator file. Follow the Simple patterns technique on page 54 or drag a pattern from the Swatches palette onto the page.

In this example, I used the *10 lpi-50%* file found in the *Pattern1.ai* library. The tile artwork will contain a bounding rectangle that is filled and stroked with None.

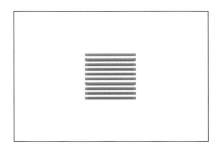

**2.** If desired, change the stroke or fill colors in the pattern tile.

In this example, I changed the stroke color to 50% black because I will be using the pattern to texturize an illustration in Photoshop.

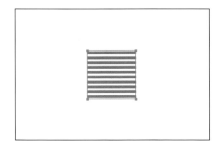

**3.** Select the bounding rectangle of the pattern tile. Choose Edit > Copy, deselect everything, and then choose Edit > Paste in Front.

If the rectangle is filled, it will cover up your tile graphics. Don't worry about that because in step 4 you will make the top rectangle into crop marks, and the fill will disappear.

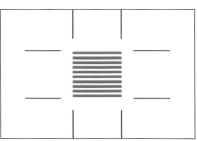

**4.** With only the rectangle selected, choose Object > Crop Marks > Make. Save the file.

In order for Photoshop to import the tile art so that it tiles perfectly, you need to create crop marks that are the same size and position as the pattern bounding box.

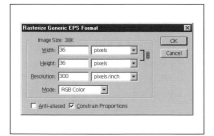

**5.** In Photoshop, open the Illustrator file you just saved. If you plan to use the pattern tile with other Photoshop files, open the file in the same mode as those files. If your pattern contains stripes or plaids at 90° angles, deselect the Anti-aliased option.

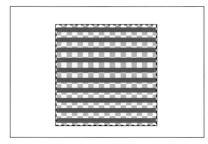

**6.** Choose Select > All to select the entire tile artwork. Then choose Edit > Define Pattern.

The pattern is now temporarily stored in memory. It will be forgotten if another pattern is defined or when you quit Photoshop.

**7.** Choose File > Save As, and save the tile with a name different from the Illustrator tile name. (Choosing Save will replace the Illustrator file with a Photoshop file.) Close the file. Create a new test file that is large enough to contain multiple pattern tiles. Be sure to open the new file in the same mode as the pattern tile.

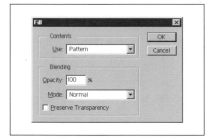

**8.** Choose Edit > Fill, and then select Pattern from the Use pull-down menu.

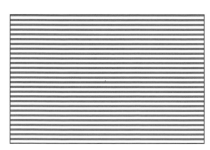

**9.** Check the overall pattern for texture and color balance. If you are satisfied with the test, the pattern is ready to use. To apply the pattern to an image, close the test file and continue with step 10.

If it isn't tiling correctly, test the original tile in Illustrator to be sure it tiled correctly there.

**10.** Open the file you want to add the pattern to.

In this example, I used an image created using the Embossed type technique on page 68. I added embossed stripes to the area around the name.

**11.** Create a new layer above all the current layers to put the pattern on. Name it *Pattern*.

**12.** Select the area you want to fill with the pattern. With the *Pattern* layer still active, click the Add Layer Mask button on the Layers palette to create a layer mask from the selection.

**13.** Click the *Pattern* layer thumbnail in the Layers palette. Choose Edit > Fill to fill the layer with the pattern.

**14.** Adjust the layer mode if necessary and add layer effects if desired. Save the file.

In this example, I set the *Pattern* layer mode to Overlay and added an Emboss layer effect to give the stripes dimension.

# Textured 3-D graphics

*Adobe Photoshop 5.0 or later*
*Adobe Illustrator 8.0 or later*

Use the Overlay mode in the Layers palette of Photoshop to easily add photographic or painterly textures to three-dimensional grayscale graphics created in Illustrator. Simply place the graphic on a layer in Photoshop. You then copy a texture onto an adjacent layer and combine the two layers using the Overlay mode. If you have several shapes to texturize, I recommend creating a separate file for each shape and then combining them in another file using flattened versions of the final texturized graphic. Don't be intimidated by the length of this technique. It's really very easy!

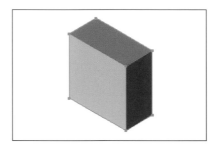

**1.** Create a three-dimensional shape in Illustrator. Paint the shape with shades of gray only. Do not use 100% black or white. Scale the artwork, if necessary, to its final size. Select all of the shapes and choose Edit > Copy to copy them to the clipboard. Save the file.

I used the Quick 3-D Boxes technique on page 8 to create this graphic.

**2.** Create a new file in Photoshop at the size and resolution you want for the final image. Choose Edit > Paste and select the Paste As Paths option. Click OK. Do not move the path from its pasted position.

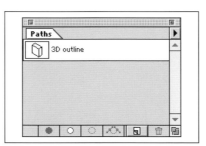

**3.** Double-click the *Work Path* name in the Paths palette and rename the path *3D outline*. Select Turn Off Path from the Paths palette popup menu.

You will use this path several times in later steps to select the outlines of the different surfaces of your object.

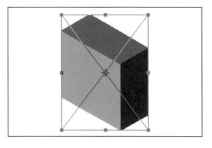

**4.** Choose File > Place, select the Illustrator file you created in step 1, and click Place. Do not move or scale the object, and it will align perfectly with the paths you pasted in step 2. Press Enter to rasterize the image.

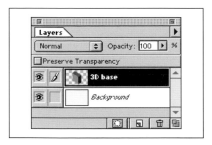

**5.** Double-click the new layer that was created by placing the graphic in step 4. Name the layer *3D base*.

**6.** Open a file with the texture that you want to appear on the surface of the three-dimensional shape. Select the area of the texture that you want to use. Use the move tool to drag the selection from its window into the *3D base* file window.

**7.** Name the new layer *Texture* and change its mode to Overlay. Option/Alt-click between the *Texture* layer and the *3D base* layer to create a clipping group of the two layers.

This is necessary so that the Overlay mode doesn't affect other layers in your file.

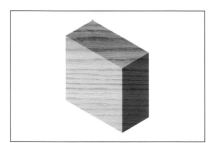

**8.** Evaluate the result. If your shape has only one visible plane, such as a cone, and you are satisfied with the result, save the file. If your shape has angled sides that need adjusting, continue with step 9.

Areas filled with 50% black will show 100% of the texture in the final artwork. Areas filled with 100% black or white will show no texture.

### Creating side surfaces

**9.** Drag the *3D base* layer thumbnail onto the New Layer button to duplicate it. Then drag the *Texture* layer thumbnail onto the New Layer button to duplicate it.

The duplicate *Texture* layer will be added to the layer group.

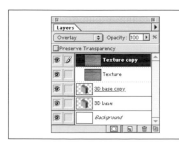

**10.** Move the *3D base copy* layer up underneath the *Texture copy* layer in the Layers palette. Recreate the clipping group with the *Texture* layer and the *3D base* layer if necessary. Rename the *3D base copy* layer *Side base*. Rename the *Texture copy* layer *Side texture*.

You should now have two separate but identical layer groups.

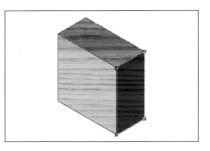

**11.** Activate the *3D outline* path in the Paths palette. Use the direct-selection tool to select the path that defines the side outline of your object.

**12.** Click the Loads path as a selection button to create a selection from the path. Choose Turn Off Path from the Paths palette popup menu so that only the selection marquee is active.

**13.** Select the *Side base* layer and click the Add Layer Mask button.

The layer mask will mask out everything but the side area of the graphic.

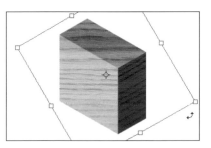

**14.** Select the *Side texture* layer and choose the move tool. Then select Edit > Free Transform. Transform the texture so that it fits naturally on the side plane of the object. Press the Return or Enter key to complete the transformation.

In this example, I rotated the wood grain so that it aligned with the edge of the side. I also scaled it a bit.

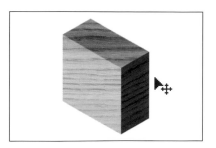

**15.** With the *Side texture* layer still selected, use the move tool to reposition the texture layer. If you are satisfied with the result, save the file. If the top plane of the shape needs adjustment, continue to step 16.

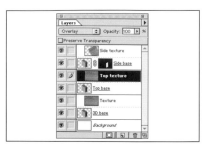

### Creating a top surface

**16.** Repeat steps 9 and 10 to duplicate the *3D base* and *Texture* layers. Rename these layers *Top base* and *Top texture*.

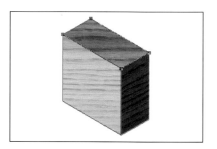

**17.** Turn on the *3D outline* path in the Paths palette. Use the direct-selection tool to select the path that defines the top outline of your object.

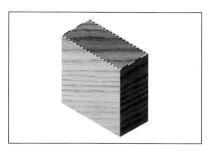

**18.** Click the Loads path as a selection button to create a selection from the path. Choose Turn Off Path from the Paths palette popup menu.

**19.** Select the *Top base* layer and click the Add Layer Mask button.

The layer mask will mask out everything but the top area of the graphic.

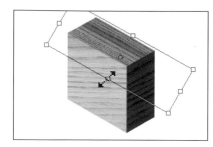

**20.** Select the *Top texture* layer and choose the move tool. Then select Edit > Free Transform. Transform the texture so that it fits naturally on the top plane of the object.

I usually scale the top texture horizontally to make it appear to recede back.

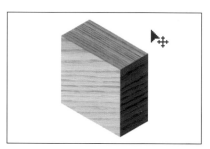

**21.** With the *Top texture* layer still selected, use the move tool to reposition the texture layer. If you are satisfied with the result, save the file. If the front plane of the shape needs adjustment, continue to step 22.

**22.** Repeat steps 11 through 15 to adjust the front plane of the object if desired. Use the *Texture* and *3D base* layers for the front planes. Repeat the entire technique for each three-dimensional shape you want to texturize.

# 4 Text Effects

# Photos masked by type

*Adobe Photoshop 5.0 or later OR*
*Adobe Illustrator 8.0 or later*

You can create type masks for photographs in Photoshop or Illustrator. Type masks are easy to create and edit in both programs, thanks to layers and grouping. However, Photoshop generates bitmapped type while Illustrator generates PostScript language outlines, so you'll need to decide which kind of output you require. If the final destination of the graphic is a Web page, use the Photoshop technique. If you are printing the graphic, use Illustrator. With both methods, heavy sans serif typefaces usually make the best-looking masks.

**Photoshop**

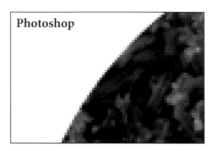

**Illustrator**

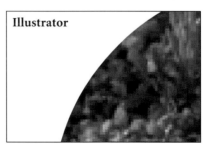

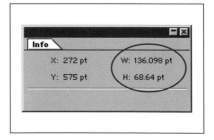

### Photoshop versus Illustrator

Before you start, decide whether you want to use Illustrator or Photoshop to create the type. Use Illustrator if you want the clean, crisp edges that PostScript typefaces and printers can deliver. Compare the edge quality of the graphics at left. Both images are shown in the same resolution. The Illustrator outline is created from Bézier curves and will always be smooth and sharp no matter what the printer or file resolution. The Photoshop edge is anti-aliased and slightly jaggy and fuzzy. There shouldn't be much difference in editability because Photoshop 5.0 has editable type layers. If your graphic will be viewed on-screen and never printed, you don't need to use Illustrator.

### Illustrator method

**1.** Open or create a new file. Select the type tool and create the type that will mask the image.

For optimal legibility of the type and image, use a large, bold face. A thin typeface design tends to lose its shape when filled with an image, and often the image within is unrecognizable.

**2.** With the type still selected, choose Window > Show Info to display the Info palette. Make a note of the width and height of the type to use in step 3.

These measurements will be helpful in determining the size your image needs to be. If it's too small, the type won't be completely filled.

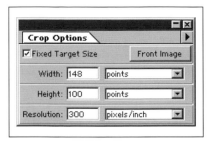

3. Switch to Photoshop and open the image you will mask with the type. Select the crop tool and set it to Fixed Target Size. Refer to the numbers you noted in step 2 and enter a width and height value that is somewhat larger than the width and height of the type. Enter whatever resolution you want.

4. Use the crop tool to select the area of the image that will be masked by type. Press the Enter key to crop the image. Save the file.

I like to keep the image about 20% larger than the type. That way I have room to reposition the image within the type once it's masked.

5. Return to the Illustrator file and choose File > Place. Navigate to the Photoshop file you saved in step 4 and click Place. While it is still selected, choose Object > Arrange > Send to Back to move the image behind the type.

In order for the type to mask the image, it must be in front of the image.

6. Select both the type and the image and choose Object > Masks > Make. If this file will be combined with other graphics, it's a good idea to group the type mask with the image. To do this, select both the type and image and choose Object > Group. Save the file.

**Photoshop method**

1. Open the image that will be masked by type.

2. Select the type tool and create the type that will mask the image.

For optimal legibility of the type and image, use a large, bold face. Thin typeface designs tend to lose their shape when filled with an image, and often the image within is unrecognizable.

3. Select the type layer in the Layers palette and move it below the image layer. The type is now hidden by the image. Option/Alt-click the line between the type and image layers to create a layer group.

Even though the layers are now grouped, you can still edit the type or move the image around.

4. Once the image is positioned within the type properly, link the layers. This allows you to move the two layers around without losing the relationship between them. Save the file.

***Variation:*** Duplicate the image layer and drag it down below the type layer so it is not part of the layer group. Create a Hue/Saturation adjustment layer and use the Colorize option to change the overall color of the image.

Link the new background file and its adjustment layer to the type layer. This maintains perfect registration between the type and the background image.

In this example, I added Layer Effects to make the type stand out. I used both Drop Shadow and Bevel and Emboss.

# Embossed type

*Adobe Photoshop 5.0 or later*

The Layer Effects feature in Photoshop 5.0 makes embossing type extremely easy and flexible. The first technique applies an emboss effect to type that retains the same color as the background layer so that it looks like it really is embossed on the background texture. After you've embossed your type, you can give it the look and feel of gold metal with the second technique. The third technique is just for fun. Use it to make chocolate bar type.

**Embossed type**

1. Open or create a file that will be the background surface for the embossed type. For best results, use a surface that contains texture. Select 50% black as your foreground color. Choose the type tool and enter your text.

2. With the type layer selected, choose Layer > Effects > Bevel and Emboss to emboss the type. Set the style to Inner Bevel and click OK.

Don't worry about the other settings too much at this point. You may want to go back and adjust them at the end of the technique.

3. Change the layer mode to Hard Light.

Hard Light mode adds shadows with the areas that are darker than 50% black, and it adds highlights with the areas that are lighter than 50% black. The main body of the type that is 50% black effectively becomes invisible.

**Gold metal embossed type**

1. Follow steps 1 through 3 for Embossed type, using a white background instead of a textured one.

**2.** Command/Ctrl-click on the type layer thumbnail to create a selection of its transparency mask. Choose Select > Save Selection to save it to a new alpha channel. Name the channel *Type mask*.

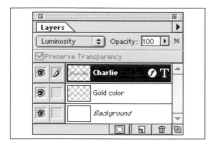

**3.** With the selection still active, create a new layer below the type layer and call it *Gold color*. Fill the selection with a gold color mix of 249 Red, 215 Green, and 121 Blue. Deselect and click on the type layer. Change its mode to Luminosity.

This mode keeps the hue and saturation of the gold type on *Gold color* with the Luminance of the embossed type layer.

**4.** With the type layer active, choose Merge Down from the Layers popup menu.

The embossed type is combined with the color type and is changed from a type and layer effects layer to a regular layer. You can now use the Lighting Effects filter in the next step.

**5.** Click on the *Type mask* channel in the Channels palette. Choose Filter > Blur > Gaussian Blur to soften the image.

This channel will be used in step 6 as a mask. More blur will produce a rounder, less beveled effect. Less blur will produce more defined bevels. I used a blur of 3 pixels in this example.

**6.** Return to RGB mode and activate the *Gold color* layer. Choose Filter > Render > Lighting Effects. Select 2 o'clock Spotlight as the Style. Choose *Type mask* as the Texture Channel.

Lighting Effects comes with a set of pre-defined lighting styles that you may want to try. I chose 2 o'clock Spotlight to ensure consistent results.

**7.** Click OK to view the results. At this point, you can add a new background or a drop shadow if desired.

In this example, I added a new background and a Drop Shadow layer effect to the metallic type.

**Chocolate bar type**

**1.** Follow steps 1 through 3 for Embossed type, using a brown background instead of a textured one. I recommend a fill of 105 Red, 50 Green, and 35 Blue.

In this example, I used Helvetica Compressed.

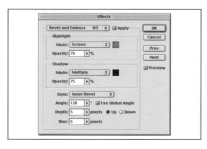

**2.** Double-click the layer effects icon on the type layer to bring up the Effects dialog box. Click on the Highlight color swatch and change it to a mix of 174 Red, 144 Green, and 117 Blue.

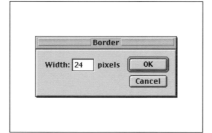

**3.** Create a new layer and name it *Border*. Choose Select > All. Then choose Select > Modify > Border. Enter a value that is twice the width of the border you want. Click OK. Choose Edit > Fill and fill the border selection with 50% gray.

**4.** Set the layer mode to Hard Light. Activate the type layer in the Layers palette. Choose Layer > Effects > Copy Effects. Then activate the *Border* layer and choose Layer > Effects > Paste Effects.

You can adjust the layer effect settings for the *Border* layer, if desired. In this example, I changed the Style to Emboss.

# Corroded type

*Adobe Photoshop 5.0 or later*

Some designers try to simulate an eroded or weathered type effect by making a series of photocopies in which each copy is made from the previous copy. The following technique lets you achieve a similar look with more control and less wasted paper. The basic technique produces a typeface with holes in it and corroded edges. The variation gives you a sketchy, scratchy look. A serif typeface design such as Times or Caslon will work well with the Eroded type technique if you want the thin parts of the letters to look eaten away.

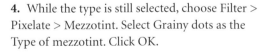

*I feel like flying
I long to be free
But Old Man Gravity
Is pullin' on me.*

**1.** Create or open the file to which you wish to add the corroded type.

**2.** Choose New Channel from the Channel palette popup menu. Select the Selected Areas option and name the channel *Type*. Click OK.

Channels are always grayscale, and they usually look like film negatives. In this technique, the channel looks like a positive grayscale image, and the areas of black and gray are the selection areas.

**3.** Press the D key to return the foreground and background colors to white and black. Then press the X key to reverse their positions. Use the type tool to create black type in the *Type* channel. Use the move tool to position the type while it is selected.

Type created in channels becomes a selection, not an editable type layer.

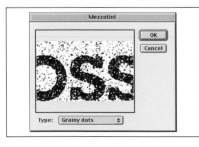

**4.** While the type is still selected, choose Filter > Pixelate > Mezzotint. Select Grainy dots as the Type of mezzotint. Click OK.

The preview proxy may show the mezzotint affecting the white area as well as the type, but as long as the type is selected, the filter will apply only to the selected area.

**5.** Deselect the type and choose Filter > Brush Strokes > Spatter. Use the proxy preview to determine the values to use for Spray Radius and Smoothness. The amount will vary depending on typeface, type size, and personal preference.

In this example, I used 48-point Lubalin Graph Demi.

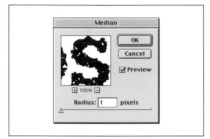

**6.** If you want to smooth out the "holes" a bit, choose Filter > Noise > Median. Turn on the Preview option and select a Radius based on how smooth and rounded you want the type to be. Then click OK.

**7.** Save the file and proceed to step 8 to add a color type layer to your artwork.

The *Type* channel is now complete and ready to be used as a selection.

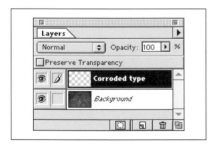

**8.** Open the Layers palette and click on the *Background* layer to view the composite color image again. Create a new layer and call it *Corroded type*.

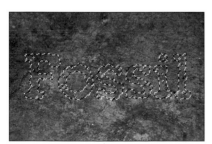

**9.** With the *Corroded type* layer still selected, choose Select > Load Selection and load the *Type* channel as the selection.

**10.** Select a foreground color to fill the type with. Choose Edit > Fill and fill the selection with the foreground color. Save the file.

If you want to change the color later, you don't need to keep loading the *Type* channel selection. Just turn on Preserve Transparency in the Layers palette for the *Corroded type* layer, and then fill. Only the non-transparent areas will be filled.

**Eroded type**

**1.** Choose a typeface design that has varied thickness in the letterforms. Follow the first technique except replace steps 4 through 6 with the following: Choose Filter > Artistic > Palette Knife. Adjust the Softness, Stroke Size, and Stroke Detail until you have the desired amount of erosion.

**2.** Choose Filter > Sketch > Torn Edges. Start with the values I've used, and then adjust them for your typeface and size.

**3.** Continue with steps 7 through 10 of the first procedure to finish the effect.

*Variation:* Follow the first technique except replace steps 4 through 6 with the following:

Choose Filter > Brush Strokes > Sprayed Strokes. Use a Vertical Stroke Direction and start with a Stroke Length of 12 and a Spray Radius of 15. Adjust these values to your taste. For a really corroded look, reapply the filter with the same settings.

# Type with multiple outlines

*Adobe Illustrator 8.0 or later*

SPECIAL EXHIBITION AT GOLDEN GATE MUSEUM

WOOD

You can create shapes with multiple outlines in Illustrator by stacking copies of the shapes on top of each other and stroking them with different colors. The last copy of the shape on the stack is filled with a color and no stroke so that only the outlines of the copies underneath appear around it. You can create this effect automatically by using the multiple outlines action in the default action set, but using my technique gives you the ability to edit the colors, line widths, and typeface easily. For help in determining line weights for the strokes, read the tip about outlining typefaces before you start.

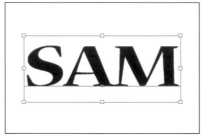

**1.** Use the type tool to create the word or letters you want to outline.

For the best results, avoid using script typefaces or specialty faces with inlines or other embellishments.

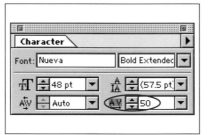

**2.** Choose Window > Show Character and enter a positive number as the Tracking value.

The amount needed varies with each typeface and the thickness of the thickest stroke. See step 11 for how to change the tracking and typestyle when you're finished.

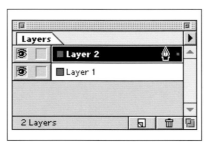

**3.** Drag *Layer 1* onto the New Layer button in the Layers palette to make a duplicate. Double-click the duplicate layer and name it *Layer 2*.

**4.** Repeat step 3 until you have one layer more than the number of outlines you want in the final artwork. Arrange the layers in numerical order.

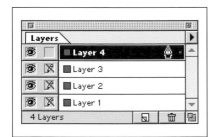

**5.** Option/Alt-click on the top layer Lock button to lock all the layers except the top one.

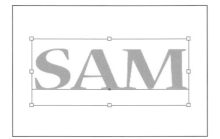

**6.** Select the type and fill it, but do not give it a stroke. The top layer should be stroked with None to maintain the integrity of the original letterform.

See the illustration at the end of this technique for more information on this.

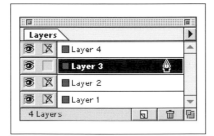

**7.** Select the layer underneath the top layer. Option/Alt-click on its Lock button to lock all layers but that layer.

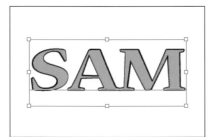

**8.** Select the type and give it a stroke.

Remember that the stroke weight you use will effectively be cut in half in your illustration. For example, I used a 1-point black stroke in this illustration, which means that you see a 0.5-point stroke in the artwork because the top layer covers up the inner half of the stroke.

**9.** Repeat steps 7 and 8 until the type on all the layers has been stroked.

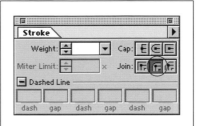

**10.** Unlock all the layers and select all of the type objects. Click the Round Join button in the Stroke palette.

Depending on the typeface design you choose, the outlines may display some odd-looking corners. Using a Round Join for the stroke corners will correct this problem.

**11.** While the type objects are still selected, adjust the tracking if necessary. You can also change the typeface and type size if desired.

Remember that if you change the type size, the stroke weights will not change, so you may need to adjust them after resizing the type.

---

### ✺ Outlining typefaces in Illustrator

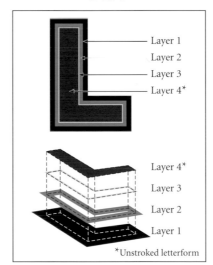

*Unstroked letterform

Before you begin, you'll probably want to determine the best stroke widths for your type outlines. When you stroke type, Illustrator creates the stroke from the center of the path that defines the outer edge of the letter. This means that a stroke value of 6 points will create a 3-point border outside the edge and a 3-point border inside it. The stroke value of each consecutive layer determines the width of the border beneath it; for example, a 4-point stroke on top of a 6-point stroke will produce a border of 1 point (6/2–4/2). You may want to do a little sketch like this one before you start so you can figure out what stroke values to use.

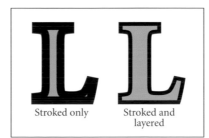

Stroked only        Stroked and layered

When stroking type, it's important to copy an unstroked version of the type on top of the stroked type to maintain the integrity and beauty of the original design. Notice how the heavy stroke eats away at the letterform in the letter that is only stroked.

# Rainbow scratchboard type

*Adobe Photoshop 5.0 or later*

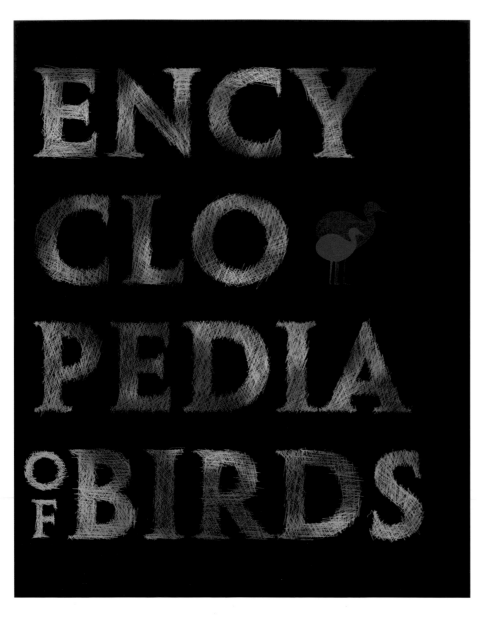

Remember when you were in grade school and you created artwork by scratching a design onto a painting covered with black wax crayon? This technique is the digital version of that style of illustration. First make a soft rainbow colored "paint" layer. Then cover it with a black layer and proceed to "scratch" away a design. You can vary my method of using outlined type as a guide and use any outlined selection. If you want your drawing to be freeform, skip making a type outline layer. Remember to use the History palette to take snapshots along the way so you can undo mistakes without losing all of your work.

**1.** Create a new file. Double-click the linear gradient tool in the toolbox to display the Linear Gradient Options dialog. Select the Spectrum gradient and fill the entire file area with the gradient.

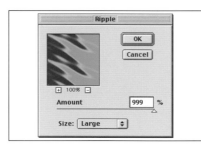

**2.** Choose Filter > Distort > Ripple to smear the colors around. Choose Large and set the Amount to 999%. Click OK.

**3.** Choose Filter > Distort > Twirl to mix up the colors even more. Set the angle at 999°.

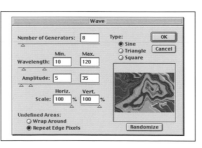

**4.** Choose Filter > Distort > Wave to distort the rainbow completely. Play with the Number of Generators option until you like the effect. Use Sine as the Type and select the Repeat Edge Pixels option. Click the Randomize button until the image is well distorted. Click OK.

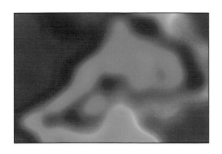

**5.** Choose Filter > Blur > Gaussian Blur to soften the colors and remove any sharp edges or abrupt color transitions. Adjust the blur amount until there are no hard edges between colors.

This makes the rainbow image look more like it was created with chalk pastels or watercolors. In this 144-ppi example, I used a blur value of 10 pixels.

**6.** Add a new layer and call it *Black*. Fill the layer with 100% black.

**7.** Add another new layer and call it *Type outlines*.

This layer will contain an outlined version of the type you will use as a guide in step 12.

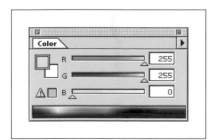

**8.** Select the type mask tool and use it to create a type selection.

**9.** Select a bright yellow color in the Color palette.

I used a mixture of R=255, G=255, B=0.

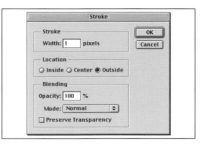

**10.** With the *Type outlines* layer selected, choose Edit > Stroke. Stroke the type with 1 pixel and choose Outside as the location. Click OK and deselect the type.

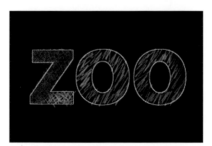

**11.** Select the Eraser tool from the toolbox. Set the erasing mode to Paintbrush and the Opacity to 100%. Select a 1-pixel paintbrush from the Brushes palette.

These are good settings to start with, but you may want to experiment with other brushes and modes when you've mastered the technique.

**12.** Select the *Black* layer and begin "scratching" the black with the eraser tool using the type outlines as a guide. Hide and show the *Type outlines* layer to view the results as you progress.

I scratched the whole letter in one direction.

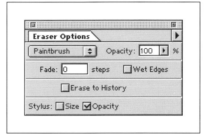

**13.** Scratch the letterforms crosswise to give them more weight and a better defined shape.

**14.** Continue to scratch away the black until you are satisfied with the result. Hide the *Type outlines* layer.

# Recessed type

*Adobe Photoshop 5.0 or later*

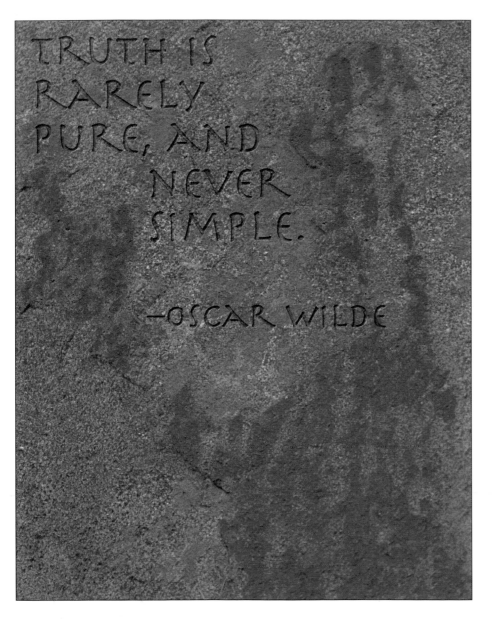

This technique makes your type look like it was engraved into a surface. You can achieve a quick cut-out effect by creating an Inner Shadow layer effect for your type. But to get it to look like it's really carved out of the surface texture, you'll need to make two more layers with layer effects. One layer creates the bevelled edge of the type cut out of the surface, and one layer adds the surface texture back into the type recess. This works well with a variety of different typefaces, but try to stay away from styles with very thin stems. Such styles tend to fill in with shadow and don't look as good as those with a more evenly distributed thickness.

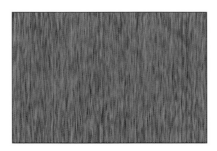

**1.** Open a file with a texture or background surface image that you want to digitally "carve" type out of. Rename this layer *Outer texture*.

In this example, I created a wood texture by running two of the Wood actions from the Photoshop 5 CD. I arranged the Pine layer on top of the Oak layer, set the Pine layer to Multiply mode, and merged the layers.

**2.** Change the foreground color to white and create the text.

If the background color is currently white, press the X key to exchange the foreground and background colors.

**3.** Choose Layer > Effects > Inner Shadow to add a cut-out effect to the type layer. Turn the Preview option on and adjust the values for your particular typestyle and letter combination. Don't click OK yet.

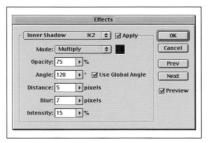

**4.** Select Inner Glow from the Effects popup menu and click the Apply button. Click on the color box next to the Mode pop-up menu and change the glow color to 100% black. Change the Mode to Multiply and set the Blur to 0. Choose Center for the glow placement. With the Preview option turned on, adjust the Opacity level until you are happy with the effect. Click OK.

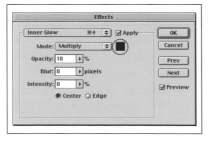

**5.** Use the move tool to adjust the position of the type against the background. The type will remain editable, but you will be making a layer mask from a selection of the type in step 7, and you won't be able to move the type around after that.

**6.** If you don't want the texture to show through the type, skip this step. Duplicate the texture layer and call it *Inner texture*. Move it beneath the *Outer texture* layer.

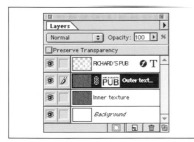

**7.** Command/Ctrl-click on the type layer thumbnail to load a selection of its transparency mask. Choose Select > Inverse to select the transparent pixels on the type layer.

**8.** Click on the *Outer texture* layer in the Layers palette and then click on the Add Layer Mask button to create a mask.

In step 9, you will add layer effects to this layer. The layer effect changes the edges of the layer. By adding a layer mask, I created "edges" of carved "wood" that I will now bevel and highlight.

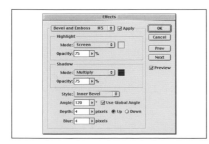

**9.** With the *Outer texture* layer still active, choose Layer > Effects > Bevel and Emboss to add a layer effect. Select Inner Bevel as the Style. Turn on the Preview option and adjust the values for your typestyle and letter combination.

You should see the edges of the texture begin to develop depth. I used a yellow highlight instead of white for a softer effect.

**10.** If you like the effect, save the file and don't continue.

You may want to readjust the layer effect settings for blur and depth on the type or texture layer. Some type styles and sizes will need more adjustment than others.

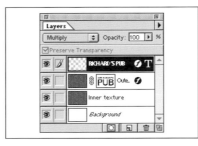

**11.** Select the type layer and change its layer mode to Multiply to reveal the texture on the *Inner texture* layer.

**12.** If you are satisfied with the effect, save the file. If desired, you can adjust the layer effects to change the size of the shadows, bevels, or highlights.

*Variation 1:* For a flat color inside the type, follow steps 1 through 10, but use a color instead of white as the foreground color in step 2.

*Variation 2:* For a colored texture inside the type, follow steps 1 through 12. Then select the *Inner texture* layer. Create a Hue/Saturation adjustment layer and group it with the *Inner texture* layer. Change the Hue, Saturation, and Lightness for the effect you want.

In this example, I used these values: Hue = −180, Saturation = −71, Lightness = −22.

# Wet paint type

*Adobe Photoshop 5.0 or later*

Bad Dog Sam

This dog is bad.
He's bad to the bone.

Making your headline or logo look like it is a puddle of readable paint is really easy with this technique. Choose a typeface that has an interesting design with swashes, swirls, and plenty of variation in the width of the strokes. Script typefaces tend to look the best. Use the Plaster filter to give the type dimension and lighting, and then colorize it with an adjustment layer. The original technique produces the type layer with its original transparency intact. If you want fatter type or eroded type, follow the variation instructions and merge the type with a background color.

**1.** Press the D key to set the foreground and background colors to black and white. Create a new file and fill the *Background* layer with 100% black.

**2.** Use the type tool to create the type that will become the "wet paint type." Select white as the type color.

The best typefaces to use for this technique are script or calligraphic. If you want a slightly eroded look, choose a face with more pronounced thicks and thins.

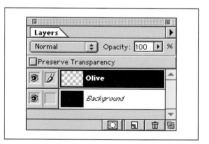

**3.** Choose Layer > Type > Render Layer to convert the editable type into pixels on a transparent background.

In order to apply filters to type, you must first render the type into pixels.

**4.** Press the X key to switch white to the foreground color. Use the paintbrush to paint drips and drops on the type layer.

I combined several brush sizes to create the drips in this example. They won't look much like drips at this point, but they will turn into small "blobs of paint" later.

**5.** Duplicate the layer that contains the text and drips to retain a copy of its transparency mask for later use. Name the new layer *Wet paint*.

**6.** With the foreground color still set to white and the *Wet paint* layer selected, choose Filter > Sketch > Plaster. Start with the values shown here for Image Balance, Smoothness, and Light Position. Adjust the values until you are happy with the proxy preview, and then click OK.

**7.** Create a new adjustment layer and select Hue/Saturation as the Type. Choose the Group With Previous Layer option so the adjustment affects only the *Wet paint* layer.

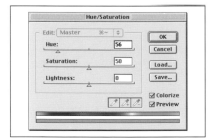

**8.** Select the Colorize option to apply color to the *Wet paint* layer. Turn on the Preview option and adjust the Hue, Saturation, and Lightness sliders until you like the way the "wet paint type" looks. Click OK.

Colorize applies color to the image while retaining the highlight, midtone, and shadow values.

**9.** Evaluate the results with the current background. If you are satisfied, save the file. You can change the color by double-clicking on the Hue/Saturation adjustment layer and altering the Hue value.

Notice that the Plaster filter maintains the original transparency mask so the type is no thicker or thinner than it was in step 4.

**Fat wet paint type**

**1.** Follow steps 1 through 5 of the first technique. Then make a duplicate of the black *Background* layer. Move it up just beneath the *Wet paint* layer.

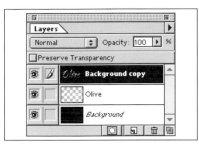

**2.** Select the *Wet paint* layer and choose Merge Down from the Layers palette popup menu.

You need to make a solid layer here because the Plaster filter needs a layer with no transparent pixels in order to spread the type and make it look fatter (or thinner).

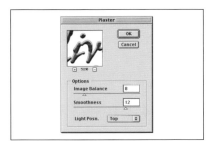

**3.** With the foreground color set to white and the *Background copy* layer selected, choose Filter > Sketch > Plaster. Start with the values shown here for Image Balance and Smoothness. Adjust the values until you are happy with the proxy preview, and then click OK.

To make the type even fatter, decrease the Image Balance or increase the Smoothness amount.

**4.** Continue with steps 7 through 9 of the first procedure to complete the process.

The result will be a solid layer with white as the background. You can remove the white, if desired, by using the selection tools or Color Range to select and delete the white. Be careful not to delete any white highlights that are within the letterforms.

*Variation:* For thinner or eroded looking type, follow the Fat wet paint type technique, but use 46 for Image Balance and 6 for Smoothness with the Plaster filter.

# Type on a circular path

*Adobe Illustrator 8.0 or later*

Illustrator does a wonderful job of setting type around a circle. But sometimes you want the type on the bottom of the circle to be positioned right side up instead of upside down. And sometimes you want the type to bend and stretch with the curve. The first technique shows you how to create type around a circle so that the type is always right side up. The second technique places type on a curved path in such a way that the type is stretched and distorted with the path. The type in the first technique retains its original shape and editability, but the type in the second technique does not.

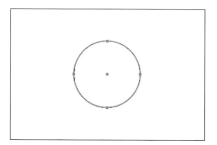

**1.** Select the ellipse tool, press the Shift key, and create a circle that defines the inside baseline of your type.

**2.** Select the path-type tool and click the top anchor point of the circle. Enter the text that you want to appear at the top of the circle.

All caps work better than upper- and lowercase letters because no ascenders or descenders bisect the arc that the letters form.

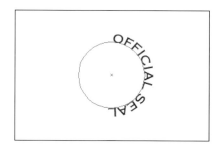

**3.** Choose Edit > Select All to select the type you just entered. Choose Type > Paragraph to display the Paragraph palette. Click the Align Center button to center the type across the top of the circle.

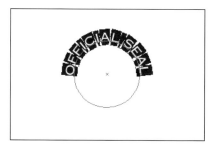

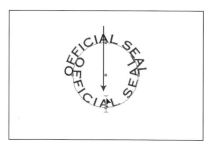

**4.** With the type still selected, choose the selection tool from the toolbox. Grab the top of the I-beam that appears in the center of the text and drag straight down, pressing the Shift + Option/Alt keys while dragging. When you get to the bottom point on the circle, release the mouse button and then the Shift + Option/Alt keys.

**5.** Select the type tool again and select all of the type on the bottom of the circle. Replace the type with the new text that you want to appear on the bottom half of the circle.

Don't worry if it overlaps the top copy; you will adjust the point size later.

**6.** Choose Edit > Select All to select all of the bottom type. Click on the Baseline Shift buttons in the Character palette to move the type so that the tops of the letters touch the edge of the circle.

Depending on the type size and design, you may have to enter a fractional amount. In this example, the baseline shift is 6.5 points.

**7.** Choose the selection tool and select both circles with their type. Click the Font Size button to adjust the type size so that it fits around the circle.

You can also adjust the letterspacing to fit the letters around the circle. In this example, I set the tracking to 40.

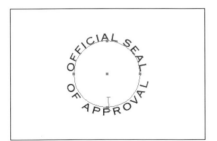

**8.** Adjust the position of the type on the circle if needed. Choose the selection tool and drag the I-beam until the type is in the desired position. Choose File > Preferences > Type & Auto Tracing and turn on the Type Area Select option to make the type easier to select.

In this example, the space between the two Ls was awkward, so I reduced it slightly.

**9.** To add a border, select the ellipse tool. Position the tool over the center point of the type circles. Option/Alt-drag from the center point outward. Press the Shift key to constrain it to a circle. Release the mouse button and then the Shift + Option/Alt keys. Repeat this step for as many borders as you want.

**Distorted circular type**

**1.** Create the type you want to apply to a curved path.

The best type style to use for this technique is bold or heavy Roman type with all caps. Italic and script faces don't work as well.

**2.** Choose Type > Create Outlines to turn the letters into paths.

The type must be turned into outlines because you will make it into an art brush in the next step. Therefore, be sure the type is correct and needs no editing before proceeding. The Create Outlines command works only with Type 1 and True Type fonts.

**3.** Choose New Brush from the Brushes palette. Select Art Brush as the brush type. Choose Hue Shift for the Colorization method. Enter a name for the brush, if desired, and click OK.

Hue Shift gives the most flexibility for changing colors. It will use whatever color the path is stroked with for the type color.

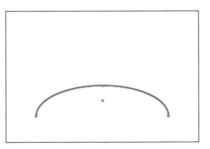

**4.** Create a curved path for the "type" art brush to be applied to. Use the pen tool to draw the curve, or create an oval or circle and delete the bottom half. Stroke the path with the color you want the type to be filled with. Use a fill of None.

**5.** With the path still selected, choose the brush you created in step 3 from the Brushes palette. Use the direct-selection tool to edit the path and change the way the type flows along it. Save the file when you are satisfied.

# Quick type effects

*Adobe Illustrator 8.0 or later*

If you are new to Illustrator and want some quick type effects for your artwork, give some of these a try. Make a drop shadow that's a darker tone of the background color. Or create a type shadow painted with a rich black that will print without showing offset registration problems. If you want to rough up your typeface, use the Tweak filter and then transform it ever so slightly to give it a rustic look. And finally, make your words overlap and appear as though they were made of semi-transparent tissue paper.

**Drop shadow (colored background)**

**1.** Select the type you want to create a shadow for. Check the view menu to see that Smart Guides is turned on.

**2.** Press the Option/Alt key and start dragging the type in the direction you want the shadow to go. Release the mouse button and then the Option/Alt key.

**3.** Choose Object > Arrange > Send Backward to place the shadow behind the type.

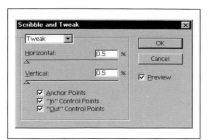

**4.** With the shadow still selected, choose the eyedropper tool from the toolbox. Click the eyedropper tool on the background color to apply that color to the shadow. Position the cursor over one of the sliders in the Color palette. Shift-drag the triangle to the right. Release the mouse button and Shift key when the shadow is dark enough.

**5.** Save the file.

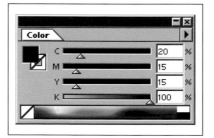

**Rich black drop shadow (white background)**

**1.** Follow steps 1 through 3 of the Drop shadow (colored background) technique.

**2.** Paint the shadow with a rich black CMYK mix.

Using all four colors instead of just 100% black will help avoid the ugly white line that appears if there are registration problems when printing.

**3.** Save the file.

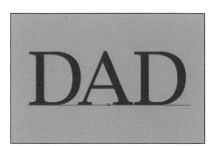

## Antiqued type

**1.** Create the type you want to "antique."

Make sure you have the final type style and copy because in step 2 you will outline the type, so it will no longer be editable.

**2.** With the type selected, choose Type > Create Outlines.

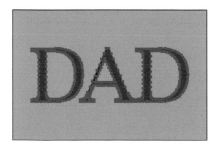

**3.** Choose Object > Path > Add Anchor Points.

Depending on the size and style of your type, you may want to repeat this step several times. The anchor points must be very close together to give the right effect in step 4. In this example, I repeated this step 3 times.

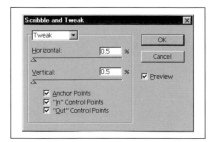

**4.** Choose Filter > Distort > Scribble and Tweak. Select Tweak from the pop-up menu and enter the same value in both the Horizontal and Vertical boxes. Use a very low value. Click OK.

For my 55-point type, I used .5%.

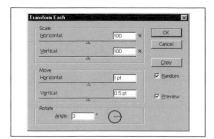

**5.** Choose Object > Transform > Transform Each. Select the Random option and set the Rotate Angle to a value between 2 and 6°. Move the letters slightly by entering different values. Check the Preview option and continue to adjust the values until you are happy with the result. Click OK.

**6.** Deselect and save the file.

If you want to apply the same treatment to a graphic, use the same steps except either skip step 2, or if you have a stroked object like in this example, select it and choose Object > Path > Outline Path. Then continue with step 3.

## Transparent type

**1.** Create the first type object and paint it.

**2.** Create the second type object and paint it. Use the selection tool to position the two type objects so that they overlap each other.

**3.** With both type objects selected, choose Type > Create Outlines.

**4.** Choose Window > Show Pathfinder to display the Pathfinder palette. With the outlines still selected, click on the Soft Mix button. Save the file.

You can make overall color changes by selecting the type and choosing Filter > Colors > Adjust Colors and adding or subtracting CMYK values.

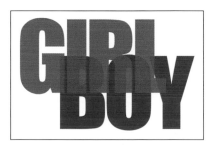

# Chrome type

*Adobe Photoshop 5.0 or later*

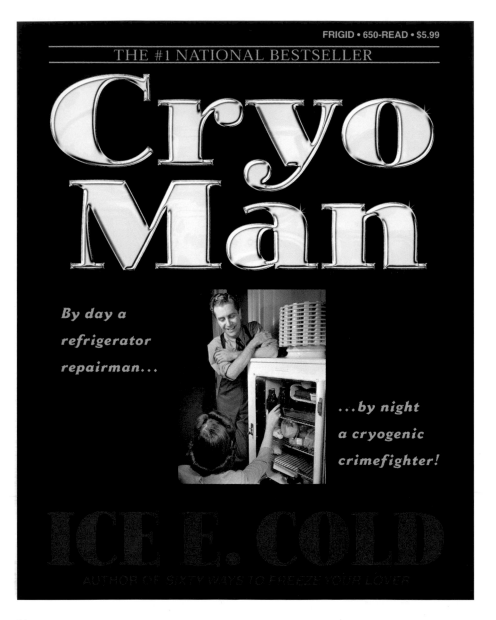

There are several ways to make chrome type using Photoshop, and most of them are fairly involved. You can do this technique in two stages. Steps 1 through 14 show you how to create embossed type that looks shiny and metallic to produce a gray type effect that can be colorized quickly with a Hue/Saturation adjustment layer. If you want to create the effect of the sky or another image reflecting off of the type, continue with steps 15 through 24. Create your own sky using the Clouds filter, or bring in another file with a sky for a different effect.

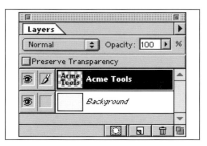

**1.** Create a new file and use the type tool to create the type that will become "chrome." Save the file and name it *Chrome type*.

**2.** Choose Layer > Type > Render layer to change the layer into regular pixels.

You can't use filters on type layers, so the layer must be rendered first. Once a type layer has been rendered, the type can be edited as pixels only, not as type.

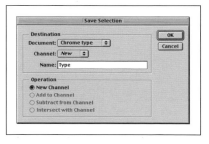

**3.** Command/Ctrl-click on the type layer thumbnail to load a selection of the type.

**4.** Choose Select > Save Selection to create a new alpha channel. Name the channel *Type* and click OK.

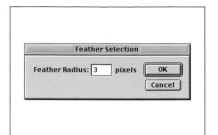

**5.** With the type still selected and its layer still active, choose Select > Feather. Choose a Feather Radius that is about 5 to 10% of the point size of your type. Remember this number because you will use it again. Click OK.

In this example, my type was 48-point so I used a 3-pixel feather.

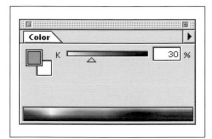

**6.** Display the Color palette and choose 30% black as the foreground color.

I selected Grayscale Slider from the Color palette popup menu to make this step easier.

**7.** With the feathered selection still active, choose Edit > Stroke to add a soft gray stroke to the inside of the type. Enter the same value you used in step 5. Select Inside as the Location. Click OK.

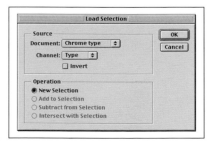

**8.** Choose Select > Load Selection and select the Type channel as the Source. Click OK.

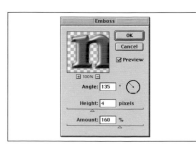

**9.** Choose Filter > Stylize > Emboss and enter an angle of 135° and an amount of 160%. Experiment with the Height amount until you like the effect. Click OK.

**10.** Choose Select > Inverse to select the area around the type. Press the Delete/Backspace key to clean up some of the soft gray pixels that remain around the edges of the type.

**11.** Choose Select > None to deselect.

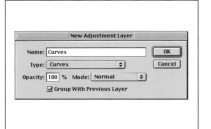

**12.** Command/Ctrl-click the New Layer button in the Layers palette to create a new Adjustment layer. Select Curves as the Type and choose the Group With Previous Layer option. Click OK.

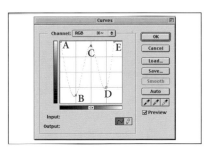

**13.** Plot the following points on the curve graph. The first number is the Input value, and the second number is the Output value.

A = 0, 255
B = 64, 31
C = 129, 238
D = 193, 63
E = 224, 255

**14.** Click OK to apply the adjustment. Save the file, and stop here if you are happy with gray chrome type. To create a distorted "reflection," continue with step 15.

If you want to stop here but want to colorize the type, add a Hue/Saturation adjustment layer, select the Colorize option and adjust the hue and saturation of the color effect.

**Adding a sky reflection**

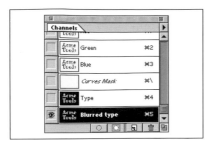

**15.** Choose Window > Show Channels to display the Channels palette. Option/Alt-drag the *Type* channel onto the New Channel button to duplicate it. Name the copy *Blurred type*. Click OK.

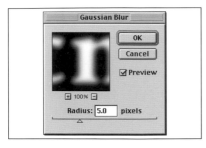

**16.** Choose Filter > Blur > Gaussian Blur. Blur the type quite a bit, using this example as a guide. Your Radius amount will vary depending on file resolution and type size. Click OK.

**17.** Choose Duplicate Channel from the popup menu on the Channels palette. Select New as the Document and name the new file *Blurred type map*. Click OK. Save the *Blurred type map* file and close it.

You will use this file with the Glass filter in step 21, so remember where you saved it.

**18.** Click on any layer in the Layers palette to reactivate the composite view of the type file. Option/Alt-click on the New Layer button to create a new layer named *Sky*.

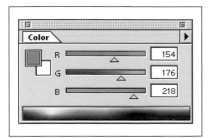

**19.** Select RGB Sliders from the Color palette pop-up menu. Choose white as the background color and blue as the foreground color. Use the blue mix that is shown here or adjust it to your own taste.

**20.** Choose Filter > Render > Clouds. To get more contrasting clouds, hold down the Option/Alt key while you choose the Clouds filter. Repeat this step until you have a cloudy sky that you like.

Each time you run the Clouds filter, the results will be different.

**21.** Choose Filter > Distort > Glass. Choose the Load Texture option from the Texture pop-up menu. Navigate to the *Blurred type map* file that you saved in step 17 and click Open. Use a Distortion of 20 and a Smoothness of 10. Click OK.

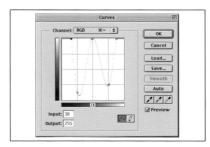

**22.** Set the *Sky* layer mode to Darken. Then Option/Alt-click on the line between it and the *Curves* layer to add it to the type layer group. If you are happy with the results, save the file. To fine-tune the contrast, continue with step 23.

**23.** Double-click the *Curves* adjustment layer icon to open the Curves dialog box. Adjust the points on the graph until you are happy with the contrast. Click OK.

This step allows you to change the thickness of the dark "reflections" around the edges of the type.

**24.** Save the file.

# 5 Special Effects

# Simulated film grain

*Adobe Photoshop 5.0 or later*

Graininess is a mottled texture created by clumps of silver on photographic film. This quality is usually seen in greatly enlarged photographs or in photographs shot with a fast film speed. This section has four techniques for adding grain to your image. Refer to the examples below to see which will work best for your image. I recommend images that have a soft, ethereal quality or subject matter for this technique. You will end up with a softer, slightly impressionistic or misty image. All of the filter values used in these examples are the same values used in the technique.

**Fine-textured grain technique (150 ppi)**

**Fine-textured grain technique (300 ppi)**

**Clumpy grain technique (150 ppi)**

**Clumpy grain technique (300 ppi)**

**Colored grain technique (150 ppi)**

**Colored grain technique (300 ppi)**

**Impressionistic grain technique (150 ppi)**

**Impressionistic grain technique (300 ppi)**

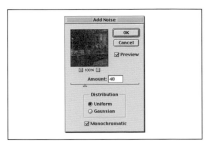

### Fine-textured graininess

**1.** Open the file you want to add grain to. Choose Filter > Noise > Add Noise. Check the Monochromatic option so that only the texture changes and not the color. Enter the desired noise amount. Click OK.

**2.** Evaluate the result and save the file.

Sometimes the fine-textured grain is quite subtle on a high-resolution file. For a more pronounced effect, try one of the following techniques.

### Colored film grain

**1.** Open an RGB file and choose Filter > Texture > Grain. Select the Enlarged Grain Type. Experiment with the Intensity and Contrast values until you are happy with the proxy preview. Click OK.

**2.** Evaluate the result and save the file.

This variation adds new colors to your image. You will see hints of pure Red, Green, and Blue values sprinkled throughout the image.

### Clumpy film grain

**1.** Open an RGB file and choose Filter > Artistic > Film Grain. Start with the values I've used here and adjust them for your image. Click OK.

**2.** Choose Filter > Noise > Median. Set the Radius to 1 pixel.

The Median filter will soften the grain and make it clumpy.

**3.** Evaluate the result and save the file.

This is a good technique to use when you want to simulate the way real photographic grain looks on a greatly enlarged image.

### Impressionistic grain

**1.** Open your file and choose Image > Mode > Lab Color. Select the Lightness channel in the Channels palette.

The Lightness channel controls the color values in the image but not the hues.

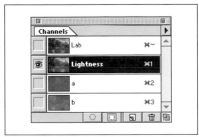

**2.** Choose Filter > Texture > Grain. Select the Clumped Grain Type. Start with the values shown here for Intensity and Contrast, and then adjust them for your image. Click OK.

**3.** Return to the Lab channel to evaluate the result. Save the file.

The resulting image is the softest and most impressionistic of all of the variations shown. Choose this method when you want the photograph to have a painterly quality but retain enough detail to look photographic.

# Posterized photographs

*Adobe Photoshop 5.0 or later*

Using the Posterize command to posterize color images can produce some unexpected results because Photoshop posterizes each channel of a color image. A two-level posterization, for example, produces two colors in each channel of an image, generating a total of eight colors in an RGB image (2x2x2). This technique gives you more control over the colors and the number of colors themselves (by converting the image to grayscale first). This technique lends itself well to process or custom color inks.

**1.** Open the image you want to posterize.

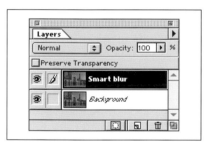

**2.** Duplicate the *Background* layer and call the new layer *Smart blur*.

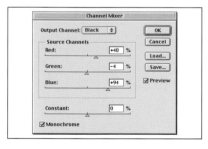

**3.** Choose Image > Adjust > Channel Mixer to remove the color from the *Smart blur* layer. Select the Monochrome option. Turn on the Preview option and move the color sliders until you have good contrast and definition of the important shapes in your image.

**4.** Choose Filter > Blur > Smart Blur to remove the detail and flatten out the gradations. Start with the Radius and Threshold values shown here, and then adjust them for your image. Set the Quality to High and the mode to Normal.

The goal here is to remove most of the texture and end up with flat shapes.

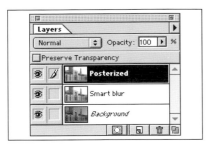

**5.** Duplicate the *Smart blur* layer and name it *Posterized* since you will now posterize this layer.

I like to save the *Smart blur* layer intact because I usually experiment with different layer modes at the end of the technique.

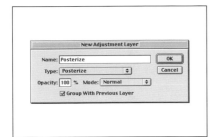

**6.** Create a new adjustment layer and choose Posterize as the Type. Select the Group With Previous Layer option to group it with the *Posterized* layer.

I use the adjustment layer instead of using the Posterize menu command because it gives me the option of experimenting endlessly.

**7.** Select the number of levels of posterization. Try different numbers to see what detail is lost or retained. The goal is to simplify the image into large flat shapes without losing critical detail. When you find the correct level, click OK.

In this example, I used 7 levels.

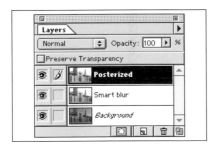

**8.** Click the New Snapshot button on the History palette to make a snapshot of the current state of the file. Then, with the adjustment layer still selected, choose Merge Down from the Layers palette pop-up menu to combine the effect with the layer.

You merge the two so you can select the shapes in step 9.

**9.** Identify areas of unwanted detail, and then select and fill them with the desired shades of gray. You can use the paintbrush tool to cover unwanted areas as well. Continue with this process until you are ready to add the color.

In this example, I filled in the white areas on the face of the building.

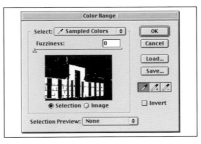

**10.** Choose Select > Color Range to select all the light gray pixels in the image. Set the Fuzziness to 0 and use the eyedropper tool to sample any light gray area in the image.

In this example, I sampled the light gray that defines the face of the building. Color Range selects all the pixels of that value.

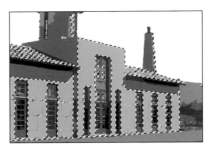

**11.** Use the Color palette to select the color you want to use in place of the gray and fill the selection with it.

For more predictable results, try to match the tonal value of the color to that of the selected gray value.

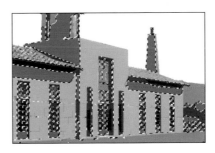

**12.** Repeat steps 10 and 11 to select a second shade of gray and change its color throughout the picture.

**13.** Repeat steps 10 and 11 until all the shapes are filled with a color. Use the pencil or paintbrush tool to retouch areas that are distracting.

In this example, I painted over the bits of texture in the foreground area.

***Variation:*** If you want an image that is a variation of tones made from one color, skip steps 10 through 13. Instead of selecting and filling the shapes with color, colorize the whole image by creating a Hue/Saturation adjustment layer. Select the Colorize option and use the Hue slider to choose the color.

# Blended image layers

*Adobe Photoshop 5.0 or later*

Photoshop offers many, many ways to blend images together. Here are three different ways using layer options, layer masks, and layer groups. Each one creates a different effect. The easiest to learn and use is the layer mask blending. Create a gradient layer mask to smoothly blend from one layer to another. If you're a more adventurous user, try playing with the layer options blending. The effects you get will depend on the images you start with and their highlight and shadow values. And if you want to mask several layers at once without having to flatten them, use the layer group technique.

**Layer mask blending**

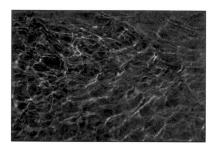

1. Open or create an image file.

2. Open another file and choose the move tool. Position the windows so that you can see both of them on screen at once. Use the move tool to drag and drop the image of one file onto the other. Press the Shift key before you release the mouse button to center the layer on top of the other layer.

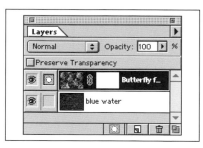

3. With the new layer still selected, click on the Add Layer Mask button in the Layers palette.

4. Select one of the gradient tools and draw a gradient on the layer mask. The white areas of the gradient will reveal the top layer, and the black areas will reveal the layer underneath. Keep redrawing the gradient until you are happy with the result.

Try different gradients and angles for different effects.

**Layer options blending**

1. Follow steps 1 and 2 of the layer mask blending technique.

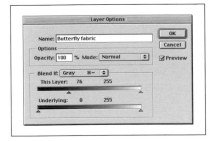

2. Double-click the layer name of the upper layer in the Layers palette to bring up the Layer Options dialog box. To drop out the darkest areas of the top layer, move the black shadow triangle on the This Layer slider to the right.

All the pixel values that fall into this range will disappear from view and reveal the layer underneath.

3. To soften the transition from layer to layer, split the shadow triangle by holding down the Option/Alt key and dragging one side away from the other. You will see two half triangles. Click OK.

The lower layer is now revealed through the darkest areas of the upper layer.

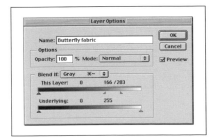

4. You can always edit and re-edit by double-clicking on the layer to get the Layer Options dialog box.

5. To reveal the lower layer in the highlight areas of the upper layer, double-click on the layer to open the Layer Options dialog box. Move the white highlight triangle on the This Layer slider to the left. Option/Alt-drag it to split it for a smoother image transition.

6. When you are satisfied with the preview, click OK.

The result shows the lower image is revealed through the lightest values of the upper image.

7. Change the layer mode of the upper layer for other blending effects.

In this example, I set the layer mode to Difference with the Layer Options set to the values used in step 5. The water texture shows through in the darker areas, and the water image shows in the lighter areas resulting in a batik-like effect.

**Layer group blending**

1. Open a file that has two or more layers. One of the layers should have a silhouette or shape that you want to use as a mask for one or more of the other layers. Position it below the layers it will mask.

In this example, I used two butterflies.

2. Option/Alt-click on the line in between each of the layers you want to group. The line becomes dotted, and the base layer name is underlined to remind you that it is the mask for the layers above it.

Once the layers are grouped with that base layer, the other layers adopt the transparency mask of the base layer.

In this example, the two layers that make the batik image created above in step 7 are masked by the two butterflies. The background image is now the lowest layer that is not part of the Layer group.

# Scanned objects as masks

*Adobe Photoshop 5.0 or later*

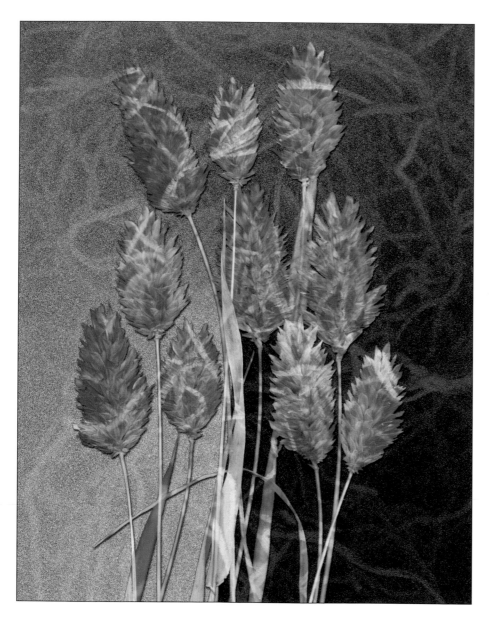

Photoshop offers many different ways to do many things and masking images is no exception. In this technique, I show you two different ways to mask an image with another scanned image. In both methods, you create a silhouette from the scanned image and use it as the mask shape. Use the clipping group method if you want to experiment with layer modes and transparency. Not only can the scanned image be used as a mask but its color and texture can also be integrated into the final effect. Use the layer mask method if you want to play with gradient blends between the image and its mask.

**Clipping group method**

**1.** Using a white background, scan the object from which you want to create the mask.

I recommend that you use a white background so that selecting it will be easy in step 3.

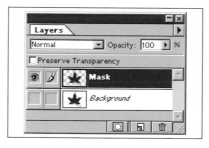

**2.** Preserve the original image by duplicating its layer. Name the layer *Mask*. Hide the original layer.

**3.** Choose Select > Color Range to select the white background around the object. Position the eyedropper tool over the white background and click. Use the other eyedropper tools to obtain a good mask of the entire white background. Click OK.

The only areas that should be selected are the ones that will NOT be part of the final mask.

**4.** If there are areas selected that are within the mask shape, deselect them now. Once you have everything outside of the mask shape selected, press Delete/Backspace to remove the pixels.

**5.** Deselect and create a new layer with the image that will be masked. Name it *Image*.

You can bring layers in from other files by either copying and pasting, or duplicating layers, or dragging and dropping.

**6.** Option/Alt-click on the line between the two layers in the Layers palette to group them.

The bottom layer in a clipping group acts as a mask for all the other layers within the group. Transparent areas will block out the image above, and the area that contains pixels will display the upper layers.

**7.** Select the move tool to adjust the way the image falls within the mask. Make the *Image* layer active and move it around until you are satisfied with the effect. Save the file.

### Layer mask method

**1.** Follow steps 1 through 5 of the Clipping group method. Command/Ctrl-click on the *Mask* layer icon to load its shape as a selection.

**2.** Select the *Image* layer in the Layers palette. Click the Add Layer Mask button to create a layer mask.

**3.** Click on the link icon between the layer mask thumbnail and the *Image* layer thumbnail to unlink the two. Click on the *Image* thumbnail.

Layer masks are linked to their layer image by default. Unlinking them allows you to move them around independently.

**4.** Use the move tool to adjust the positioning of the image within the layer mask. Once you are satisfied with their relationship, relink them by clicking between their thumbnails in the Layers palette again.

Keep the layer linked with its mask so you can move the two as a group.

***Variation 1:*** To maintain some of the texture and color of the *Mask* layer image, click on the *Image* layer and set the mode to Color.

***Variation 2:*** Follow steps 1 through 4 of the Layer mask method. Load the *Mask* layer as a selection. Click on the layer mask thumbnail of the *Image* layer.

The selected area will be the only area of the layer mask that will be affected in the next step.

Select the gradient tool and create a gradient within the selection. When you are satisfied with the effect, deselect and save.

The gradient on the layer mask creates a smooth blend between the image on the *Mask* layer and the image on the *Image* layer.

# Halftone with image dots

*Adobe Photoshop 5.0 or later*

A halftone image is created by converting a continuous tone image into dots of various sizes. The halftone dot can be any shape or size. It can even be a line. In this technique, I use an image as the halftone dot. If the dot image is a color one, the halftoned image takes on the dot color scheme. I try to keep the dot large enough that you can see the image of the dot but small enough that it reproduces the main image well. Experiment with different blending modes and layer modes to create some fun effects.

**1.** Open the RGB image that you want to halftone.

Images that contain well-defined and recognizable shapes work best with this technique. Don't use images that depend on texture or fine details because those will disappear in the halftoning process.

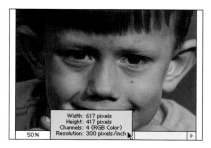

**2.** Option/Alt-click on the file size box in the lower-left area of the document window and make a note of the width (in pixels) and resolution of the image.

You will use this information in a later step to calculate the size of the halftone dot.

**3.** Option/Alt-drag the *Background* layer onto the New Layer button to duplicate it. Name the layer *Gray image*.

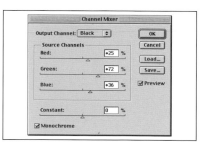

**4.** Choose Image > Adjust > Channel Mixer to remove the color from the *Gray image* layer. Turn on the Preview option and the Monochrome option. Adjust the three channel values until the preview shows a well-balanced grayscale version of the original color image.

Your image may require different Source Channel values depending on its tonal range.

**5.** Click OK to convert the layer to a grayscale image.

This layer will be used to define the tonal values of the final image.

**6.** Open the image that will be used as the halftone dot.

This image can be a photograph, type, scanned object, or digital painting. You can use a logo or graphic as well.

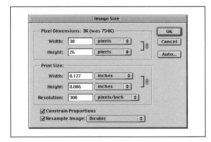

**7.** Choose Image > Image Size to reduce the size of the dot file. Enter the resolution of the other file that you noted in step 2. Divide this resolution by the number of image dots per inch that you want in the final image. Enter this value as the Pixel Dimensions Width.

Because I wanted 8 dots per inch, I divided 300 dpi by 8 and got 37.5. So I entered 38 as my width.

**8.** Choose Select > All to select the entire dot image. Choose Edit > Define Pattern to save the pattern tile in Photoshop's pattern memory.

**9.** Activate the final image file again and create a new layer called *Pattern*.

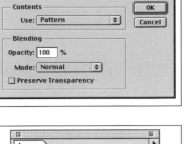

**10.** Choose Edit > Fill to fill the layer. For the Contents, choose Pattern from the pull-down menu. Click OK.

**11.** Duplicate the *Pattern* layer to retain a copy of the original pattern.

Step 12 requires the use of the Apply Image command, which will permanently alter the contents of the *Pattern* layer. It's best to make a copy of it in case you want to experiment with other settings and modes.

**12.** Choose Image > Apply Image to combine the *Pattern copy* layer with the *Gray image* layer. Set the Blending to Overlay and turn on the Preview option to see if you like the results.

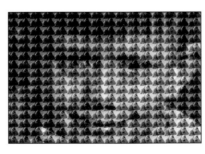

**13.** Once you are happy with the results, click OK and save your file.

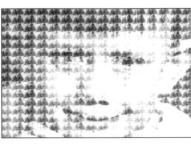

*Variation:* Try a different blending mode in step 12. In this example, I used the Add mode.

# Brushstroke masks

*Adobe Illustrator 8.0 or later*

Cropping an image with a mask made of brushstrokes can make the image look as though it were painted on the page. If you don't have time to actually paint a shape on paper, scan it, and then use it as a mask; you can manufacture one in Illustrator. Using the paintbrush tool and several of the paintbrush designs from the Illustrator CD, create a "painted shape" out of several paintbrush strokes. Then turn them into shapes and join them into one large mask shape. Because it is a path, it can be edited or transformed at any time. Look on page 94 for a similar technique using Photoshop.

**1.** Choose File > Place to place the image you will be masking.

You can link or embed the image file, depending on your needs. To keep my file size small, I chose to link this image.

**2.** Make a rough sketch of the shape of the frame you want. Use the pencil tool to outline the general area of the image you wish to reveal.

**3.** With the path still selected, choose View > Make Guides.

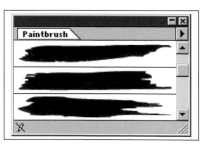

**4.** Choose Window > Brush Libraries > Other Library to open another brush library. Open the Adobe Illustrator CD, choose Illustrator Extras > Brush Libraries > Artistic, and open *Paintbrush.ai*.

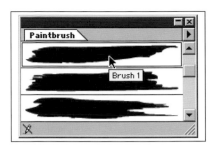

**5.** Select the paintbrush tool from the toolbox. Then choose *Brush 1* from the Paintbrush palette you just opened. Be sure the fill color is set to None and the stroke is set to black.

**6.** Create a brush stroke using the guides as an indicator of where to stop and start the stroke.

I angled my stroke in this example for a more painterly look.

**7.** Make another brush stroke next to the previous one.

Be sure not to get too close, or the paintbrush will redraw the first line you made. To ensure you are starting a new stroke, look at the cursor. You should see a paintbrush icon with an "X" next to it.

**8.** With the last stroke still selected, choose a new brush from the Paintbrush palette. Using different brushes varies the edge of the frame.

In this example, I chose *Brush 2*.

**9.** If the stroke doesn't overlap the previous stroke well or if it doesn't cover the area the way you want, redraw it. Position the paintbrush over the path and recreate the stroke. Repeat steps 7 and 8 until the entire guide shape is filled.

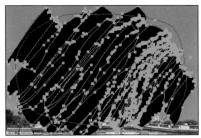

**10.** Select all the paintbrush paths you created and choose Object > Expand. Select the Stroke option and click OK.

Expand turns the stroke into a filled shape. The original path is left attached to the shape, but it is filled and stroked with None. In order to use the shapes as masks, you need to remove those paths.

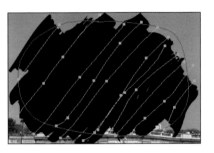

**11.** Using the direct-selection tool, select the path you created in step 6. Then choose Edit > Select > Same Paint Style. Delete these paths. They are no longer needed.

**12.** Select all the paintbrush shapes.

If you have several paths or if they are very complex and large, select just three or four paths.

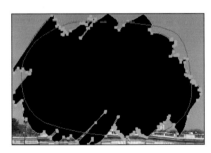

**13.** Choose Window > Show Pathfinder to display the Pathfinder palette. Click the Unite button to join the selected paths into one. Remove any little shapes that fall inside or outside the main large path.

Repeat steps 12 and 13 as many times as necessary to unite all the brush shapes into one shape.

**14.** With the large paintbrush shape still selected, Shift-select the image. Choose Object > Masks > Make to apply the paintbrush mask to the image. Save the file.

If nothing appears after making the mask, you need to go back to step 13 and remove all the extra shapes that are grouped with the mask.

# Reverse shapes

*Adobe Illustrator 8.0 or later*

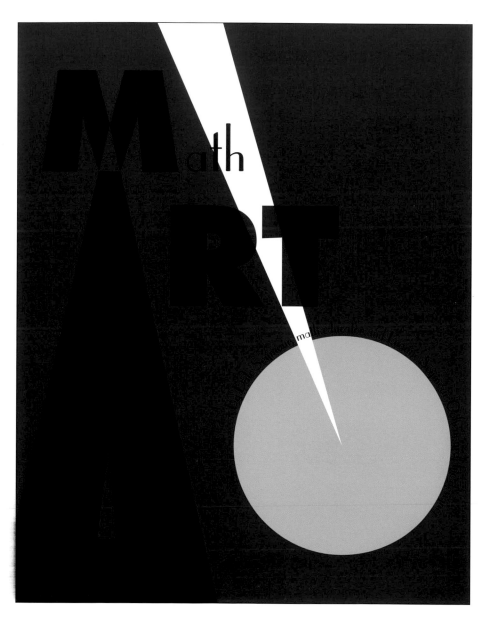

The effect of overlapping type and graphics is common in Art Deco graphic design. You can use these techniques, however, for any overlapping shapes whose colors you want to change at the point where the shapes overlap. If you want to be able to move the shapes after creating the reversed effect, use the Compound Path method. If you want to paint shapes with different colors, use the Pathfinder technique.

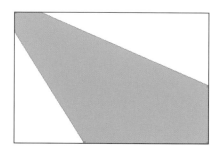

**Compound path technique**

**1.** Create the background element of your design.

Keep in mind that the paint attributes of the backmost object will be adopted by the other objects in the compound path.

**2.** Create the objects or type that will be reversed out of the background element. Position them as you want them in the final design.

**3.** If you are not using type as an element, skip this step. If you are using type, select it and choose Type > Create Outlines.

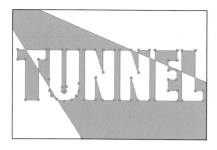

**4.** Select the background element and the foreground type or elements. Choose Object > Compound Paths > Make.

**5.** Deselect everything and check your work. Place an element behind the compound path and notice that you can see through the "holes" that were created in the background element of the compound shape.

In this example, I placed a black rectangle behind the compound path.

**6.** Use the direct-selection tool to adjust elements of the compound path.

You can move, reshape, or transform the objects within the compound path. If you try to change the color, though, it will change for the entire compound path.

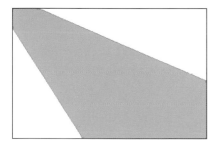

**Pathfinder technique**

**1.** Create the background element of your design.

The paint attributes of this object will be changed to that of the topmost object after you use the Pathfinder command in step 4.

**2.** Create the objects or type that will be reversed out of the background element. Position them as you want them in relation to the background element; after step 4, you won't be able to readjust the position of the elements.

**3.** If you are not using type as an element, skip this step. If you are using type, select it and choose Type > Create Outlines.

**4.** Select the background element and the foreground type or elements. Choose Window > Show Pathfinder to display the Pathfinder palette. Click the Exclude button.

The Exclude command knocks out any overlapping areas of color between the objects. To create all solid shapes with no "holes," click the Divide button instead of Exclude.

**5.** Use the direct-selection tool to select the objects you want to repaint and change as desired.

Each remaining area of color is now a separate object, and you can no longer move the original artwork elements. The overlapping areas that look white are actually "holes" in the artwork.

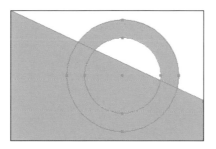

**Compound path problems**

You may find that some objects are solid that you wanted to be transparent or vice versa. Usually these objects were already compound paths before you compounded them again. To correct this problem, you must reverse the direction of these paths.

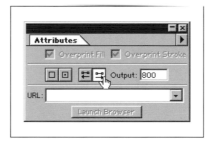

Use the direct-selection tool and select one of the paths that isn't reversing properly. Choose Window > Show Attributes. Click the Reverse Path Direction button that is not selected. Continue selecting and changing directions until the artwork is displayed correctly.

In this example, I changed the directions on both circles before it was displayed properly.

# Filter combinations

*Adobe Photoshop 5.0 or later*

Sometimes you want a texture or special effect that can't be achieved with the application of just one filter. Shown here are just a few of the hundreds of combinations you can use to enhance images. Although these examples illustrate filters applied to the entire image, these combinations can also be applied to just a selected area. To create an effect shown here, apply the filters in the order indicated. Note, however, that the effect may vary with different image resolutions and modes.

Original 300 ppi images.

### Blur & Diffuse

**1.** Choose Filter > Blur > Gaussian Blur. Use a Radius of 2.0 pixels.

**2.** Choose Filter > Stylize > Diffuse. Use Normal mode and apply the filter three more times.

### Mosaic & Ripple

**1.** Choose Filter > Pixelate > Mosaic. Use a Cell size of 10.

**2.** Choose Filter > Distort > Ripple. Use Medium size at 100%.

### Pointillize & Facet

**1.** Choose Filter > Pixelate > Pointillize. Use a Cell size of 5.

**2.** Choose Filter > Pixelate > Facet. Apply the filter two more times.

## Pointillize & Glass

**1.** Choose Filter > Pixelate > Pointillize. Use a Cell size of 6.

**2.** Choose Filter > Distort > Glass. Use a Distortion of 1 and Smoothness of 2. Select Frosted as the Texture and leave the Scaling at 100%.

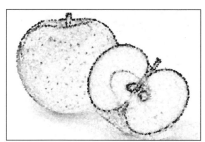

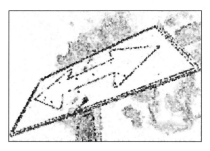

## Find Edges & Crystallize

**1.** Choose Filter > Stylize > Find Edges.

**2.** Choose Filter > Pixelate > Crystallize. Use a Cell size of 6.

## Poster Edges & Smart Blur

**1.** Choose Filter > Artistic > Poster Edges. Use an Edge Thickness of 4, an Edge Intensity of 2, and a Posterization of 3.

**2.** Choose Filter > Blur > Smart Blur. Use a Radius of 40 and a Threshold of 68. Set the Quality to High and the mode to Normal.

## Graphic Pen & Palette Knife

**1.** Set the foreground color to Black. Choose Filter > Sketch > Graphic Pen. Set Stroke Length to 15, Light/Dark Balance to 50, and Stroke Direction to Right Diagonal.

**2.** Choose Filter > Artistic > Palette Knife. Set Stroke size to 2, Stroke Detail to 3, and Softness to 7.

## Dry Brush & Graphic Pen

**1.** Choose Filter > Artistic > Dry Brush. Set Brush size to 7, Brush Detail to 8, and Texture to 1.

**2.** Set foreground color to Black. Choose Filter > Sketch > Graphic Pen. Set Stroke Length to 15, Light/Dark Balance to 50, and Stroke Dir. to Right Diag.

**3.** Choose Filter > Fade Graphic Pen. Set the mode to Soft Light at 100%.

# 6 Web techniques

# Animation along a path

*Adobe Illustrator 8.0 or later*
*Adobe ImageReady 1.0 or later*

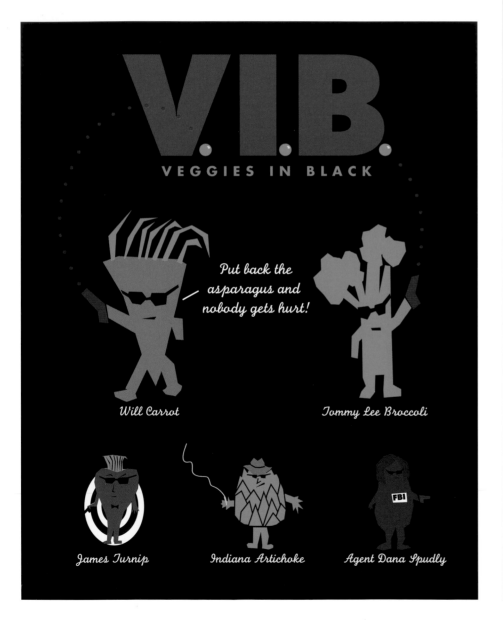

With the scatter brush tool, Illustrator offers the ability to paint an image along a path. You can use this tool to create artwork for an animation that moves along that path. First create the path, and then paint the path with the scatter brush. Then create layers for each of the frames you want in your animation. Using ImageReady, simply open the layered file and create the animation without enhancing it. You can make it even smoother with tweening in ImageReady, but the file may be larger and it will take a little bit more work.

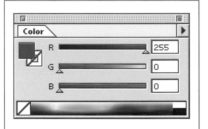

**1.** In Illustrator, open a new file. Choose Window > Show Color to display the Color palette. Choose RGB from the Color palette pop-up menu.

Because this animation will be viewed on a Web page, you'll get better color results if you paint with RGB values.

**2.** Create the object that you want to move along a path in your animation.

If you are copying the object from existing artwork, convert the colors to RGB by selecting it and choosing Filter > Colors > Convert to RGB.

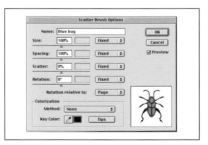

**3.** Choose Window > Show Brushes to display the Brushes palette. Select the artwork and choose New Brush from the Brushes palette pop-up menu. Select Scatter Brush as the type. Name the brush and leave the other settings at their default values. Click OK.

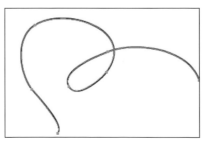

**4.** Use the pen or pencil tool to create the path you want your graphic to move along. Draw it in the direction you want the object to move.

For example, I wanted my bug to start at the bottom of the page so I started the path there.

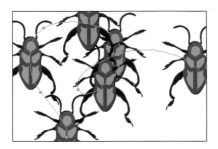

**5.** With the path still selected, select the scatter brush you just made from the Brushes palette.

Don't panic. It probably doesn't look too great right now. We will finesse the art in the next few steps.

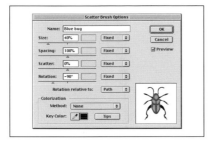

**6.** Double-click on the scatter brush thumbnail in the Brushes palette to open the Options dialog box. Turn on the Preview option and change the Size and Rotation until the object is placed along the path in the correct position and size.

I changed the Rotation to -90°, and I set Rotation relative to Path so my bug would face the direction the path was drawn.

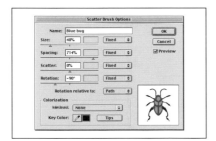

**7.** Start increasing the Spacing amount and watch the previewed artwork. When you can see only one object at the beginning of the path, you have the correct spacing. Click OK.

If you push Spacing to 1000% and still have more than one object on the path, your path may be too long. Split the path into shorter segments and follow steps 7 through 11 for each segment.

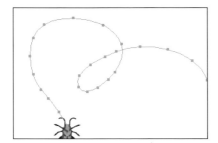

**8.** Choose Object > Path > Add Anchor Points. Repeat this step two or three times.

In a later step, you will remove parts of the path as the object travels along it. The more points along the path, the more positions the object can have, and thus the more steps in your animation. If you want a lot of steps, add a lot of points.

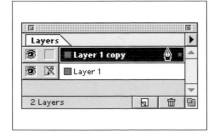

**9.** Choose Window > Show Layers to display the Layers palette. Drag *Layer 1* onto the New Layer button to duplicate it. Lock *Layer 1*.

The duplicated path on the new layer will automatically be selected. Each layer will eventually become a frame in the animation.

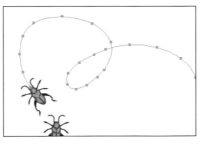

**10.** Identify the point on the path where you want the object to appear in the next animation frame. Use the direct-selection tool to select the part of the path between that point and the first point on the path. Delete the selected points.

Because the bug is always centered on the first point of the path, it has now moved up along the path.

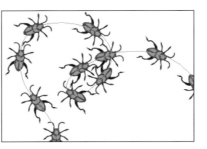

**11.** Repeat steps 9 and 10 until you have the number of layers (frames) you want for your animation. Save the file.

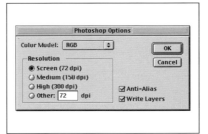

**12.** Choose File > Export to export the file for use in ImageReady. Give the filename a *.psd* extension. Select RGB as the color model and Screen as the resolution. Turn on the Anti-Alias and Write Layers options. Click OK.

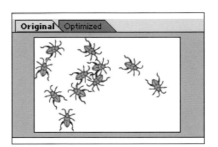

**13.** Start ImageReady and open the exported *.psd* file.

All the layers will be retained in the file. In this example, I had 11 layers, one for each bug that was visible.

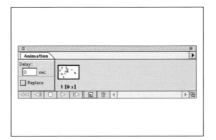

**14.** Choose Window > Show Animation to display the Animation palette. The first frame of the animation will appear as selected and current. Click the Duplicate Current Frame button to make a copy of the first frame. Repeat this until you have the same number of frames as layers. Select frame 1 when you are finished.

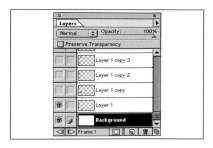

**15.** If the Layers palette is not open, choose Window > Show Layers to display it. Hide all the layers except *Layer 1* and *Background*.

Option/Alt-click on the eyeball icon to quickly hide all layers but that one or to show all layers including that one. The way your file looks now will be frame 1 of the animation.

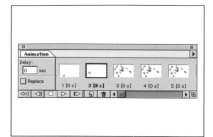

**16.** Select frame 2 in the Animation palette.

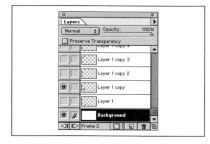

**17.** Hide *Layer 1* and show *Layer 1 copy* in the Layers palette.

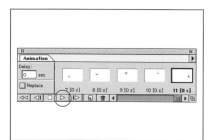

**18.** Repeat steps 15 through 17 until you have one frame for each layer in the file. Click the Play Animation button at the bottom of the Animation palette.

You should see a fast version of the scatter brush object travelling along the path over and over again.

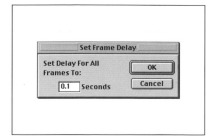

**19.** Choose Set Delay For All Frames from the Animation palette popup menu. Enter the number of seconds you want each frame viewed. Click OK. Click the Play button again to test the animation.

Because my animation subject is a bug, I used a fairly fast pace.

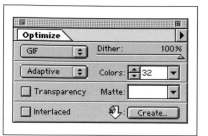

**20.** Choose Window > Show Optimize to display the Optimize palette. Select GIF as the file format and Adaptive as the Color Reduction Algorithm. Click the Optimize tab at the top of the image window. Continue reducing the colors until you have the desired image quality and file size. Choose File > Save Optimized As to save the GIF animation.

**Tweening for smoother animations**

**1.** Follow steps 1 through 18 of the first technique. Select Frame 2 and show the *Background*, *Layer 1*, and *Layer 1 copy* layers.

Tweening creates extra frames between two frames. The movement must all take place on one layer, so you'll use the other layers as guides.

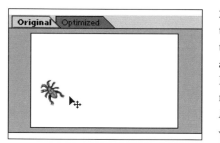

**2.** Select *Layer 1* in the Layers palette. Choose the move tool from the toolbox and reposition the object on *Layer 1* so that it approximately aligns with the object on *Layer 1 copy*. Choose Edit > Free Transform and rotate the object if necessary. Once the objects are aligned, hide *Layer 1 copy*.

You can now tween between frames 1 and 2.

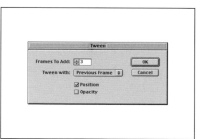

**3.** With frame 2 selected, choose Tween from the Animation palette popup menu. Turn on the Position option and select Previous Frame from the Tween pop-up menu. Select the number of frames you want to add and click OK.

ImageReady automatically adds the extra frames between frames 1 and 2.

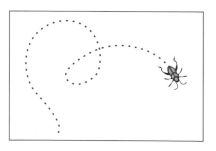

**4.** Repeat steps 1 through 3 of this technique for each of the frames you want to tween between. Finish the file with steps 19 and 20 of the first technique when you are finished tweening.

This example shows the animation in flat form. Since I can't show motion in a book, the dotted line illustrates the movement of the bug.

# Custom browser-safe colors

*Adobe ImageReady 1.0 or later*

Many people are still viewing Web sites using 8-bit color displays, which means that the illustration or Web graphics you create may have some drastic color shifts. If it is critical that you control the color shift of an illustration or logo, consider making your own browser-safe "custom color" with a custom dither pattern. You'll be using Web-safe colors to create dither patterns that simulate other, more subtle or sophisticated colors that seem otherwise unattainable. Using this method, you can keep your files small, be certain that the colors won't shift, and get colors that come closer to the original design.

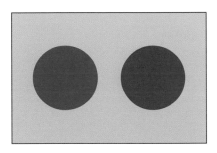

**1.** Create a graphic for your Web page in Photoshop or Illustrator. Put different colored objects on different layers for easy selection. If you create it in Illustrator, export the file as Photoshop 5 format with the Write Layers option turned on.

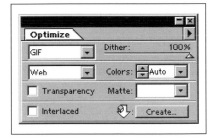

**2.** Choose Window > Show Optimize to display the Optimize palette. Select GIF as the file format and Web as the Color algorithm.

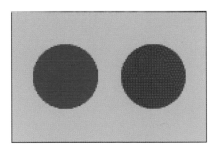

**3.** Click on the Optimize window tab to see what the image will look like in GIF format with Web colors.

In this example, the coral color has a distracting dither, the green is too yellow, and the tan background has a reddish cast.

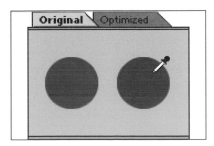

**4.** Return to the Original view of the image and select the eyedropper tool from the toolbox. Position the eyedropper over one of the problem colors and click to make that color the foreground color.

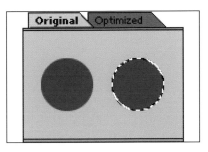

**5.** Use one or more of the selection tools to select the area filled with the problem color.

In this example, I created each shape on a separate layer so that selection would be easy. Using Command/Ctrl-click on the layer thumbnail, I quickly selected the shape.

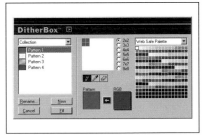

**6.** Choose Filter > Other > DitherBox.

Notice that the foreground color you sampled is displayed in the lower-right box labeled RGB. Whatever pattern was used last is displayed in the Pattern box.

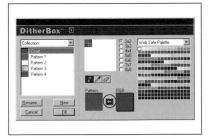

**7.** Make sure that Web Safe Colors/Palette is selected in the upper-right pop-up menu. Click the arrow between the Pattern and RGB boxes to create a new dither pattern that approximates the sampled color. If you want to name the color, click the Rename button to change its default name. Fill the selection in the image by clicking the Fill button.

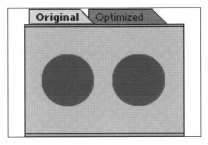

**8.** Click the Optimized window tab to view the change. Repeat steps 5 through 7 for other problem colors in the file. When you're satisfied with the colors, choose File > Save Optimized to save the GIF file for use in a Web page.

# Efficient large images

*Adobe Photoshop 5.0 or later*
*Adobe ImageReady 1.0 or later*

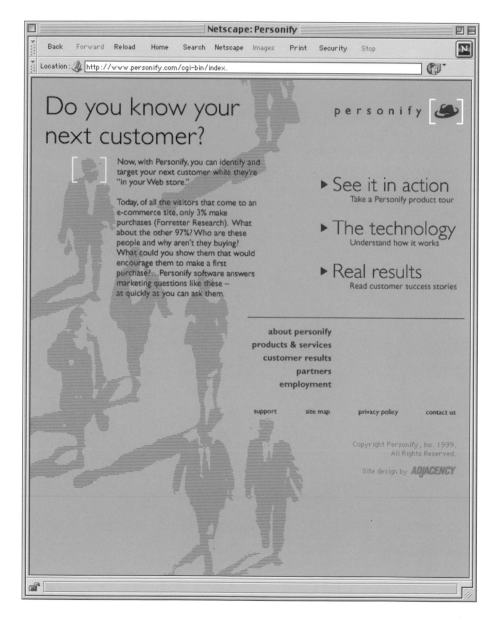

Large images can be very difficult to use on Web sites because the file size causes long download times. But Web designers don't have to sacrifice the graphic impact of full-screen images if you prepare the image using this technique. Images saved in GIF format compress to very small sizes if you create them with flat colors and a stripe pattern. First, posterize the image to reduce its colors. Then add a stripe pattern both as a graphic effect as well as a means of reducing the file size. Finally, optimize the image using ImageReady. Choose images that have strong contrast for this technique.

**1.** Open the image you want to use as a background in your Web page. Choose File > Save As and save the file under a different name to preserve the original.

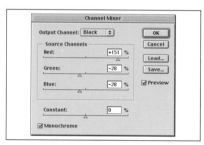

**2.** Choose Image > Adjust > Channel Mixer. Select the Monochrome option to remove the color. Turn on the Preview option and adjust the sliders until the grayscale image has good contrast and edge definition.

The edge definition is important because in step 3 you will posterize the image and lose much of the detail.

**3.** Choose Image > Adjust > Posterize and enter 2 as the number of levels. Turn on the Preview option to view the result. Click OK.

If important areas of the image drop out, click Cancel and use the dodge or burn tool to increase the contrast. Then try to posterize again.

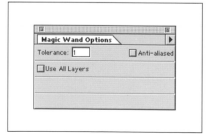

**4.** Double-click the magic wand tool in the toolbox to select it and open the Magic Wand Options palette. Set the Tolerance to 1 and turn off the Anti-aliased option.

**5.** Position the magic wand in one of the white areas of the image and click. Then choose Select > Similar to select all the rest of the white pixels in the image.

**6.** Select a foreground color and Option/Alt+ Delete/Backspace to fill the selection with the foreground color. Choose Select > Deselect.

**7.** Repeat steps 5 and 6 for the black areas of the image. Save the file. Choose the eyedropper tool and sample one of the two colors in the file. This color will be the stripe color.

**8.** Choose File > New and create a new file that is 1 pixel wide by 2 pixels tall. Match the resolution of the other file. Select Transparent for the Contents. Click OK.

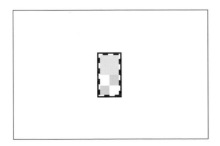

**9.** Zoom in on the file and select the pencil tool from the toolbox. Choose a 1-pixel brush and click once on the top pixel of the file to add one pixel of the foreground color. Save the file and name it *1 Pixel stripe*. Choose Select > All and then Edit > Define Pattern to store the 2-pixel image as a pattern.

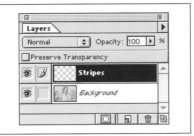

**10.** Return to the large image file and Option/Alt-click on the New Layer button to create a new layer. Name the layer *Stripes*. Click OK.

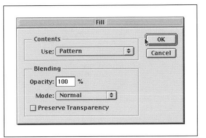

**11.** With the *Stripes* layer still selected, choose Edit > Fill and select Pattern from the Use pop-up menu. Click OK.

**12.** Evaluate the result. If you aren't happy with the color cast that the stripes have created, repeat steps 9 through 11, using a different color for the stripe. If you are happy with the result, choose File > Save a Copy, give it a new name, and select the Flatten Image option when you save it.

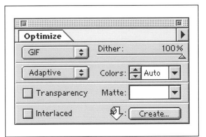

**13.** Start ImageReady and open the file you just saved. Choose Window > Show Optimize to display the Optimize palette. Choose GIF as the file format.

**14.** Click on the Optimized tab in the window to view the result. Change the options in the Optimize palette until you are satisfied with both the image quality and the file size. Choose File > Save Optimized and save the GIF file for use in your Web page.

In this example, my file went from 83.2K before optimization to 6.4K after optimization.

# Shortcuts and handy tips

*Adobe Photoshop 5.0 or later*
*Adobe Illustrator 8.0 or later*
*Adobe ImageReady 1.0 or later*

As stated in the introduction, you should have a basic knowledge of the software and its tools, commands, and palettes before you try the techniques. But I realize that you are busy and overwhelmed and can't always remember all the commands and shortcuts, so this appendix contains most of the basic shortcuts that you'll need to efficiently use techniques in this book. Refer to the Quick Reference Card that came in your software box for a complete listing of all the keyboard shortcuts.

| | Photoshop and ImageReady | | Illustrator | |
| --- | --- | --- | --- | --- |
| | **Windows** | **Macintosh** | **Windows** | **Macintosh** |
| **Forget what's what?** | Choose File > Preferences > General > Show Tool Tips | | Choose File > Preferences > General > Show Tool Tips | |
| **Repeat a task** | | | | |
| Reselect last selection | Shift+Ctrl+D | Shift+Command+D | — | — |
| Use last Levels settings | Alt+Ctrl+L | Command+Option+L | — | — |
| Apply last filter | Ctrl+F | Command+F | Ctrl+E | Command+E |
| Display last filter dialog | Alt+Ctrl+F | Command+Option+F | Alt+Ctrl+E | Option+Command+E |
| Transform with copy | Alt+Ctrl+T | Command+Option+T | Hold down Alt key | Hold down Option key |
| Transform again | Shift+Ctrl+T | Shift+Command+T | Ctrl+D | Command+D |
| Transform again with copy | Shift+Alt+Ctrl+T | Shift+Command+Option+T | Use Ctrl+D/Command+D (if copy was made originally) | |
| **Moving selected objects** | | | | |
| Constrain movement to 45° or angles set in Prefs | Shift | Shift | Shift | Shift |
| Leave a copy behind | Alt+move tool | Option+move tool | Alt+selection tool | Option+selection tool |
| **Speeding up painting** | | | | |
| Select background color (eyedropper) | Alt+click a pixel | Option+click a pixel | — | — |
| Select foreground color (eyedropper) | Click an image pixel | Click an image pixel | — | — |
| Fill with foreground color | Alt+Backspace | Option+Delete | — | — |
| Fill with background color | Ctrl+Backspace | Command+Delete | — | — |
| Get eyedropper while painting | Alt | Option | — | — |
| Display Fill dialog box | Shift+Backspace | Shift+Delete | — | — |
| Paint with straight line (any painting tool) | Click-Shift-Click | Click-Shift-Click | — | — |
| Return to default colors | D key | D key | D key | D key |
| Switch colors of fill/stroke | X key | X key | X key | X key |
| Toggle between eyedropper and bucket tools | Alt | Option | Alt | Option |
| Create tint | — | — | Shift-drag color slider in Color palette | |
| Fill/stroke with None | — | — | / key | / key |
| Apply color to selection with eyedropper tool | — | — | Double-click any object | Double-click any object |
| Select paint attributes with eyedropper tool | — | — | Click on an object | Click on an object |
| Sample intermediate color in gradient (eyedropper) | — | — | Shift+click on gradient object | Shift+click on gradient object |

## Frequently used shortcuts for the Layers palette

| Shortcut | Macintosh/Windows keystrokes |
|---|---|
| **All three products** | |
| Create and name new layer | Option/Alt-click on New Layer button |
| Delete selected layer | Option/Alt-click on the Delete/Trash button |
| Duplicate new layer | Drag layer onto New Layer button |
| Show/hide just one layer | Option/Alt-click on eye column of that layer |
| Show/hide multiple layers | Drag through the eye column |
| **Photoshop** | |
| Create new adjustment layer | Command/Ctrl-click on New Layer button |
| Disable layer effect temporarily | Option/Alt-click on the Layer Effects icon |
| Make mask on an adjustment layer | Make selection and fill with black |
| View mask on an adjustment layer | Option/Alt-click adjustment layer thumbnail |
| View layer mask | Option/Alt-click the layer mask thumbnail |
| **Photoshop and ImageReady** | |
| Center layer dragged from another file | Press Shift while dragging layer into window |
| Combine visible layers onto new layer | Create new layer; Option/Alt+Merge Visible |
| Create layer mask from selection | Make selection; click Add Layer Mask button |
| Create layer with a selection | Command/Ctrl+J |
| Discard/apply a layer mask | Drag layer mask thumbnail to Trash button |
| Duplicate and name new layer | Option/Alt-drag layer onto New Layer button |
| Group with the layer below | Command/Ctrl+G |
| Make/release a clipping group | Option/Alt-click on line between layer names |
| Move several layers at once | Link the layers before moving with move tool |
| Select layer's transparency mask | Command/Ctrl-click on the layer thumbnail |
| Turn on/off a layer mask temporarily | Shift-click the layer mask thumbnail |
| **Illustrator** | |
| Copy selection onto a different layer | Option/Alt-drag selection dot to other layer |
| Display all but active layer in artwork mode | Command+Option/Ctrl+Alt-click eye icon |
| Select several contiguous layers | Shift-click on the layer names |
| Select several non-contiguous layers | Command/Ctrl-click the layer names |
| Select everything on layer | Option/Alt-click on the layer name |
| Toggle preview and artwork mode | Command/Ctrl-click on eye column |
| Unlock all/lock all but one layer | Option/Alt-click on lock column of that layer |

## Frequently used shortcuts for the Layers palette

**Photoshop Layers palette**

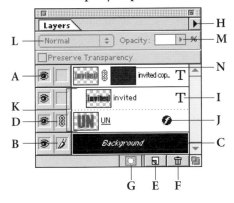

**ImageReady Layers palette**

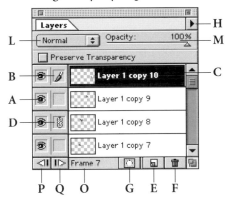

**Illustrator Layers palette**

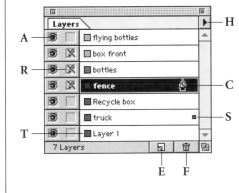

The following letters correspond to the palette images:

**A.** Show/Hide
**B.** Selected layer icon
**C.** Active layer
**D.** Link/Unlink
**E.** New Layer button
**F.** Delete Layer button
**G.** Add Layer Mask button
**H.** Displays popup menu
**I.** Type layer icon
**J.** Filter effects icon
**K.** Layer group
**L.** Layer mode
**M.** Layer opacity
**N.** Layer mask
**O.** Current animation frame
**P.** Previous animation frame
**Q.** Next animation frame
**R.** Lock/Unlock
**S.** Current selection in artwork
**T.** Layer selection color

# Combining Photoshop and Illustrator files

The fact that Photoshop is raster-based and Illustrator is vector-based is important to take into consideration when you're sharing artwork between the two programs. *Raster-based* means that objects are described as pixels on a raster, or grid. As a raster-based program, Photoshop is better for working with organic shapes, such as those in photographs or paintings. *Vector-based* means that objects are mathematically described as points connected by straight or curved lines. Vector-based graphics generated in Illustrator have crisp, clear lines when scaled to any size.

## *Bringing Photoshop files into Illustrator*

There are four different ways to bring Photoshop files into Illustrator: the Place command, drag-and-drop, copy and paste, or the Open command. I don't recommend the drag-and-drop or copy and paste methods because the image is converted into a 72 ppi, RGB image. However, you can copy paths created in Photoshop and paste them into an Illustrator file with no loss of image quality. The pasted paths will always be filled and painted with None, however.

### The Place command

In Illustrator, choose File > Place and turn on the Link option if you want to link the file; turn off the option if you want to embed the file. The advantages to linking are that the file size stays small, and, although you can't use filters on the linked images, you can update the image using the Links palette.

### The Open command

In Illustrator, choose File > Open and select the Photoshop image. Illustrator creates an embedded image and enables you to use the Photo Cross Hatch, or Object Mosaic filters on it. Unfortunately, embedded images become part of the Illustrator file and increase its file size.

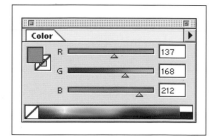

### *Bringing Illustrator artwork into Photoshop*

Here's a way to avoid color shift problems when you know you'll be using an Illustrator file in Photoshop: Create the file using RGB colors. If necessary, you can convert the colors to RGB by selecting the objects and choosing Filter > Colors > Convert to RGB.

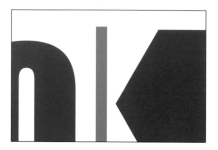

### Raster versus Vector

Before using Illustrator graphics in Photoshop, evaluate the artwork. Decide whether you want your shapes and type to have sharp, clean edges like the illustration at left. If so, leave the artwork in Illustrator.

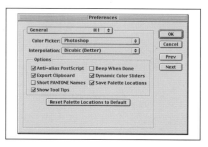

When you open an Illustrator file in Photoshop, it rasterizes the vector-based Illustrator file, removing all layering and grouping and transforming the crisp curves into pixels. Minimize the "stair-stepping" on curves by selecting the Anti-alias PostScript option in the Photoshop General Preferences dialog box. (By default, this option is on.)

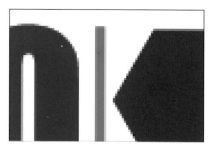

Anti-aliasing can make the edges of objects appear fuzzy. It is generally preferable to the "stair-stepping" appearance that occurs without it. Note that the thick green line is not improved by anti-aliasing.

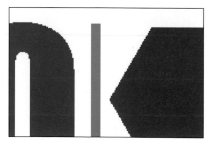

On the other hand, if your artwork consists of vertical and horizontal lines and no curves, you can achieve better results without anti-aliasing.

| Bringing Illustrator files into Photoshop | | | | |
|---|---|---|---|---|
| Command/Action | Procedure | Advantages | Disadvantages | Notes |
| Copy and paste commands | 1. Copy type, paths, or graphic objects in Illustrator to the Clipboard.<br>2. Switch to Photoshop.<br>3. Paste the copied item.<br>4. Choose Paste As Pixels or Paste As Paths. | 1. You don't need to save separate files.<br>2. Pasting paths allows you to make precise graphic selections and objects in Photoshop. | You can't scale the pasted item until after Photoshop has rasterized it, which causes degraded image and edge quality. | Photoshop creates a new layer and rasterizes pasted objects at their size in the Illustrator file. |
| Export command | 1. In Illustrator, show all the layers you want to export.<br>2. Choose File, Export and select Photoshop 5 as the format.<br>3. Name the file and click Save to get the Photoshop Options dialog box.<br>4. Choose Color Model and Resolution.<br>5. Turn on the Write Layers option.<br>6. Turn on Anti-alias unless the graphics are all horizontal and vertical lines.<br>7. Open the file in Photoshop. | Photoshop keeps all the layers separated. Only the areas where objects reside have pixels; the surrounding areas are transparent, which makes for easy selection and manipulation. | Hidden layers won't appear in the Photoshop file. | Photoshop adds a white-filled Background layer to the file. |
| Open command | 1. In Photoshop, choose File > Open and select the Illustrator file.<br>2. Use the Rasterize dialog box to make the resolution of the new file match that of any Photoshop image you'll be combining with the open Illustrator file.<br>3. Rename the rasterized file when saving. | This method works best with complete page designs. | 1. Photoshop crops the Illustrator image to the outermost bounding box of the artwork.<br>2. Photoshop flattens the layers into one. | |
| Place command | 1. In Photoshop, choose File > Place.<br>2. Shift-drag the highlighted corners of the box to scale the image proportionally. | 1. You can easily transform graphics and type before rasterizing to avoid quality loss.<br>2. The imported image has no background pixels and adapts to the resolution of the current Photoshop file. | | Photoshop doesn't rasterize the image until you press the Return/Enter key. |

# Recommended Reading

ADOBE DEVELOPMENT TEAM. *Adobe Illustrator 8.0 : Classroom in a Book* (The Classroom in a Book Series). San Jose, CA: Adobe Press, 1998.

ADOBE DEVELOPMENT TEAM. *Adobe Photoshop 5 Classroom in a Book*. San Jose, CA: Adobe Press, 1998.

ADOBE DEVELOPMENT TEAM. *Print Publishing Guide*. San Jose, CA: Adobe Press, 1998.

ALSPACH, TED, PIERRE BEZIER. *Illustrator 8 Bible*. Foster City, CA: IDG Books Worldwide, 1999.

BIEDNY, DAVID, BERT MONROY, NATHAN MOODY. *Photoshop Channel Chops*. Indianapolis, IN: New Riders Publishing, 1998.

BLATNER, DAVID, BRUCE FRASER. *Real World Photoshop 5* (Real World Series). Berkeley, CA: Peachpit Press, 1999.

CAMERON, JULIA. *The Artist's Way*. New York, NY: Tarcher/Putnam, 1992.

DAVIS, JACK, SUSAN MERRITT. *The Web Design Wow! Book*. Berkeley, CA: Peachpit Press, 1998.

DAY, ROB. *Designer Photoshop*. New York, NY: Random House Electronic Publishing, 1995.

DAYTON, LINNEA, JACK DAVIS. *The Photoshop 5 Wow! Book*. Berkeley, CA: Peachpit Press, 1999.

DINUCCI, DARCY, MARIA GUIDICE, LYNNE STILES. *Elements of Web Design, 2nd Edition*. Berkeley, CA: Peachpit Press, 1998.

GREENBURG, ADELE DROBLAS, SETH GREENBURG. *Fundamental Photoshop 5*. Berkeley, CA: Osborn McGraw-Hill, 1998.

HARPER, TALITHA, SARA BOOTH. *Step-By-Step Electronic Design Techniques*. Berkeley, CA: Peachpit Press, 1998.

HAYNES, BARRY, WENDY CRUMPLER. *Photoshop 5 Artistry*. Indianapolis, IN: New Riders Publishing, 1998.

LOPECK, LISA, SHERYL HAMPTON, PATRICK AMES. *Adobe Seminars: Web Page Design*. Indianapolis, IN: Hayden Books, 1997.

MCCLELLAND, DEKE, KATRIN EISMANN. *Photoshop Studio Secrets, 2nd Edition*. Foster City, CA: IDG Books Worldwide, 1999.

MCCLELLAND, DEKE. *Real World Illustrator 8*. Berkeley, CA: Peachpit Press, 1998.

MCCLELLAND, DEKE. *Photoshop 5 Bible*. Foster City, CA: IDG Books Worldwide, 1998.

MCCLOUD, SCOTT. *Understanding Comics*. New York, NY: HarperCollins, 1993.

MONROY, BERT, DAVID BIEDNY. *Adobe Photoshop: A Visual Guide for the Mac*. Reading, MA: Addison Wesley Publishing Company, 1996.

MULLET, KEVIN, DARRELL SANO. *Designing Visual Interfaces*. Mountain View, CA: SunSoft Press, 1995.

SALLES, DENISE, GARY POYSSICK, ELLEN BEHORIAM. *Adobe Photoshop Creative Techniques*. Indianapolis, IN: Macmillan Computer Publishing, 1996.

SIEGEL, DAVID. *Creating Killer Web Sites, Second Edition*. Indianapolis, IN: Hayden Books, 1997.

STEUER, SHARON. *The Illustrator 8 Wow! Book*. Berkeley, CA: Peachpit Press, 1999.

TUFTE, EDWARD R. *The Visual Display of Quantitative Information*. Cheshire, CT: Graphics Press, 1983.

WEINMAN, LYNDA. *Coloring Web Graphics*. Indianapolis, IN: New Riders Publishing, 1997.

WEINMAN, LYNDA. *Designing Web Graphics 3*. Indianapolis, IN: New Riders Publishing, 1999.

WEINMANN, ELAINE, PETER LOUREKAS. *Illustrator 8 for Windows and Macintosh* (Visual Quickstart Guide Series). Berkeley, CA: Peachpit Press, 1999.

WEINMANN, ELAINE, PETER LOUREKAS. *Photoshop 5 for Windows and Macintosh* (Visual Quickstart Guide Series). Berkeley, CA: Peachpit Press, 1998.

WILLMORE, BEN. *Official Adobe Photoshop 5.0 Studio Techniques*. Indianapolis, IN: Adobe Press, 1998.

XENAKIS, DAVID, SHERRY LONDON. *Photoshop 5 In Depth*. Scottsdale, AZ: Coriolis Books, 1998.

# Index

# Credits

| | |
|---|---|
| Author: | Luanne Seymour Cohen |
| Book Design/production: | Sandy Alves |
| Production Assistant: | Suzanne Yamada |
| Cover Design: | Michael Mabry |
| Back Cover Photo: | Jeff Schewe |
| Executive Editors: | Chris Nelson |
| | Steve Weiss |
| Development Editors: | Barb Terry |
| | Jennifer Eberhardt |
| Technical Editor: | Gary Kubicek |
| Copy Editor: | Audra McFarland |
| Indexer: | Cheryl Jackson |
| Testers: | Sandy Alves |
| | Lisa Trail |
| | Jessica Helfand |
| | Jeffrey Tyson |

# Photography and illustration credits

All photography and illustration was done by Luanne Seymour Cohen unless noted in the chart below. Italics indicate large focal illustrations.

| Photographer/Artist | Page number(s) |
|---|---|
| Adjacency | *110* (web site) |
| Sandy Alves | 6 *(map)*, 114 (scarecrow) |
| Artbeats | 63 (wood) |
| Classic PIO Library | 93 (fabric) |
| Katrin Eismann | 88, 110 |
| Aren K. Howell | *92* |
| Hung Yin-Yin | *72* |
| Illustrator 8 CD brush library | 48 (box), 106 (bug) |
| Julieanne Kost | *66, 90, 94* |
| PhotoDisc | 18, 28, 39, 46, 59, 60, 62, 84, 95, 96, 97, 102 |
| Unknown | 38 (woman) |

**Colophon**

This book was designed and produced using Adobe PageMaker 6.5, Adobe Illustrator 8.0, and Adobe Photoshop 5.0 on a Power Macintosh G3 computer. The Adobe Original Minion and Minion Expert typefaces are used throughout the book.